G000230076

RYA
navigation exercises

2003

Authors
Chris Slade and Sara Hopkinson

Photographers: Patrick Roach • Christel clear
Bluegreen • Gary Blake

Illustrator: Sarah Selman

Charts reproduced by kind permission of
the UK Hydrographic Office • Nautical Data Ltd
Imray Laurie Norie & Wilson Ltd

Published by
The Royal Yachting Association
RYA House Ensign Way Hamble
Southampton SO31 4YA

Tel: 0845 345 0400
Fax: 0845 345 0329
Email:info@rya.org.uk
Web: www.rya.org.uk

Foreword

Welcome to the RYA Navigation Exercises book which aims to help you become more competent, knowledgeable and therefore safer at sea.

The use of electronic navigation aids such as GPS and electronic chart plotters is becoming widespread. However, a sound grasp of the principles of traditional navigation is essential for those using electronic equipment - for safety reasons, should the equipment fail, but also to make use of the full benefit of the electronic aids. This book encompasses a range of navigational techniques for both paper charts and electronic navigation equipment.

These exercises, written by the authors of the RYA assessment papers, provide an opportunity to hone the skills learnt on RYA Shorebased courses. Being able to answer these questions means that you have reached the level of the theory part of the Yachtmaster Offshore examination. I hope you will also find them an interesting challenge.

Chris Slade and Sara Hopkinson are both highly experienced RYA Instructors and Examiners under sail and power, and fully understand the reality of converting shorebased course knowledge into practical skippering.

James Stevens FRIN
RYA Training Manager and Chief Examiner

Introduction

These RYA Navigation Exercises have been designed and written to help improve your seamanship and navigation skills, and to complement the RYA Dayskipper and Coastal Skipper/Yachtmaster shorebased courses.

The questions become progressively harder, going from Dayskipper through to Yachtmaster level, as you work through each chapter.

Everything you need to answer the questions will be found at the back of the book, including two RYA Training Charts. No other charts, pilot books or almanacs are necessary.

However, if you would like more background reading, we recommend the new *RYA Navigation Handbook*.

We hope you enjoy these exercises.

Chris Slade and Sara Hopkinson
August 2003

The RYA Practice Navigation Charts 1 and 2 included with this book have been designed for practise use only. They must, on no account, be used for actual navigation.

Equipment needed

Course plotter (Breton, Portland, Douglas protractor, parallel rule etc).

Dividers (large), 2B pencils, soft eraser.

Navigational precision

At sea, it is often impracticable or even undesirable to work to high levels of precision, but at times the safety of the yacht depends on precise navigation and accurate calculations. The exercises assume the latter and the questions require a navigational precision of 0.1 mile and 0.1 metre for tidal calculations.

Abbreviations

M	Nautical Miles
m	metres
(T)	True
V	Variation
(M)	Magnetic
D	Deviation
(C)	Compass

Contents

Extracts

Exercises

Seamanship 1

1.1

a) Which tack is this yacht on?

b) Which buoy is on the leeward bow?

c) Which arrow is marking the port quarter?

d) Which buoy is on the port bow?

e) Which arrow is showing the starboard beam?

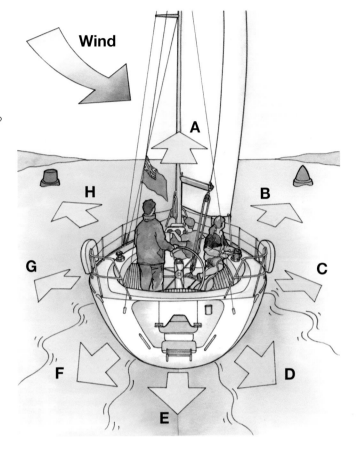

1.2

a) What type of knot is this?

b) What are some of its uses?

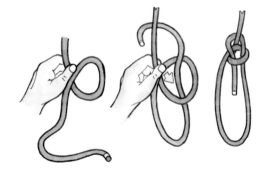

1.3

a) Name each anchor.

b) Which type of anchor has poor holding in sand and mud?

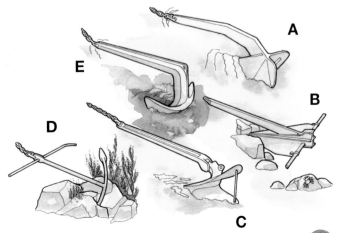

1.4

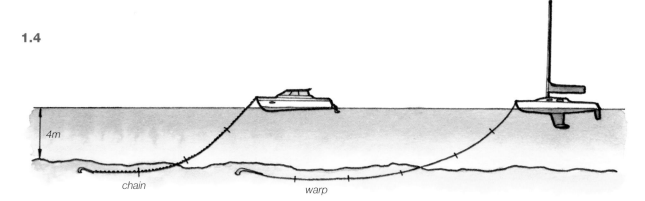

4m

chain   *warp*

These boats are anchored in 4 metres of water.

    a)   What length of anchor chain does the motor cruiser require?

    b)   The yacht is using a minimum amount of chain and then warp. What total length is necessary?

    c)   What type of rope is best for anchor warps? Why?

    d)   When anchored what signal are they required to display during the day? Why is it important to follow this rule?

    e)   What is the signal at night?

1.5

Suggest 4 factors to consider when choosing an anchorage.

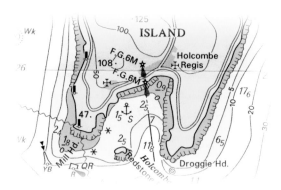

1.6

    a)   What is a rolling hitch used for?

    b)   Which way will it not slide, to the right or to the left?

Chart familiarisation 2

Use RYA Chart 2

2.1

Complete the following:

    a)   Meridians of .... run from pole to pole dividing the world into segments.

    b)   Parallels of .... run round the world north and south of the Equator.

2.2

Which letters refer to the following?

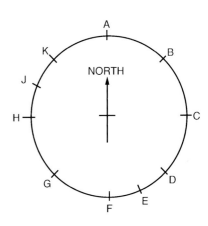

    i)   090°   v)   270°

    ii)   135°   vi)   315°

    iii)   180°   vii)   225°

    iv)   000°   viii)   045°

2.3

Complete the following:

    a)   1 degree (1°) of Latitude or Longitude = ... minutes.

    b)   1 minute of Latitude (1') = 1 ....

    c)   1 nautical mile per hour of speed on a boat = 1 ....

2.4

What are the meaning of the following chart symbols?

    a)   b)   c)   d) e)    f)

2.5

What features are in the following positions?

    a)   50°13'.5N   004°28'.3W

    b)   50°23'.3N   004°29'.6W

    c)   50°26'.0N   004°24'.4W

    d)   50°10'.25N   004°24'.5W

    e)   50°14'.1N   004°37'.0W

    f)   50°19'.9N   004°33'.2W

2.6

What is the TRUE bearing and distance from the Skerries Point lighthouse
(50°14'.45N 004°29'.8W) to:

    a)   The unlit red buoy in position 50°16'.3N   004°33'.7W?

    b)   The green buoy marked FL.G.5s in position 50°16'.2N   004°27'.5W?

    c)   The South Walton south cardinal buoy in position 50°13'.05N   004°28'.7W?

    d)   Start Point lighthouse in position 50°13'.3N   004°38'.5W?

2.7

What features are in the following positions?

    a)   216°(T) from Berry Head lighthouse 3.7 miles?

    b)   302°(T) from Berry Head lighthouse 2.7 miles?

    c)   033°(T) from Berry Head lighthouse 3.9 miles?

    d)   151°(T) from Berry Head lighthouse 3.15 miles?

2.8

In what book can details of all the symbols that are used on Admiralty charts be found?

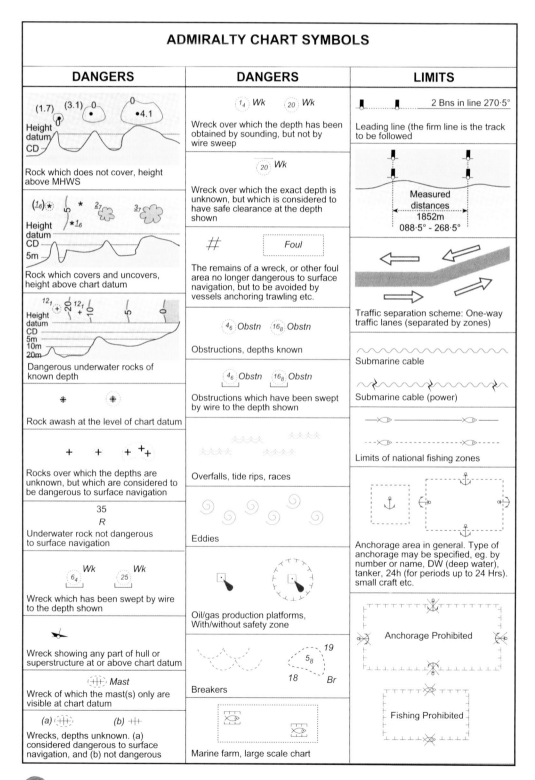

Compass & position fixing

Use RYA Charts 1 and 2
Use variation 7°W on Chart 1 and 6°W on Chart 2

3.1

What is the magnetic variation on **RYA Chart 1** in 2004 to the east of Falmouth?

3.2

What is the **MAGNETIC** bearing for each of the following:

    a)   240°(T)   variation 4°E

    b)   050°(T)   variation 7°W

3.3

What is the **TRUE** bearing for each of the following:

    a)   130°(M)   variation 3°E

    b)   348°(M)   variation 7°W

3.4

    a)   What is compass deviation?   b) What are some of the possible causes?

3.5

At slack water, a vessel approaching Saint Helier is lined up with the leading lights, 082°(T).
If the boat's steering compass reads 095°(C), what is the deviation on this heading?

3.6

At 1230 the following bearings were taken while to the east of Dartmouth:

Kingswear chimney	268°(M)
Berry Head lighthouse	355°(M)
Small building on Crabrock point	301°(M)

At the time the bearings were written in the logbook, the depth was 49.2m. Plot the fix.

3.7

At 0920 while motoring south passed South Coombe Island the GPS gives the position as
50°14'.1N 004°26'.7W. The skipper notes this in the logbook and plots the position on the
chart.

What observations can be made to check this?

3.8

While on passage towards Dartmouth the navigator sees that the chimney and day beacon at
Kingswear will come into transit and plots this on the chart. The transit occurs at 1724 and at
the same time the bearing of the church tower at Stoke Fleming is 285°(M). Plot the fix.

3.9

A skipper is navigating on passage towards Salcombe using the GPS. The centre of the compass rose south of South Coombe Island has been put into the GPS as a waypoint to make plotting positions quicker than using latitude and longitude. The GPS gives a continuous display of the direction and distance to the waypoint.

At 1538 the direction and distance to the waypoint is displayed as 204°(T) 1.4 miles.

Plot this position on the chart. How can this position be confirmed?

3.10

At 2100 the skipper of a boat to the southeast of Grand Lejon lighthouse (bottom left-hand corner of **RYA Chart 1**) takes the following bearings:

Grand Lejon	314°(M)
Rohein	198°(M)
Cap Frehel	102°(M)

Depth reduced to soundings 20.5 metres.

On plotting the bearings, the skipper is dismayed to find the fix is unreliable with a large cocked hat.

a) What is the most likely reason for the poor quality of the fix?

b) How could the skipper reduce the area of probability within the cocked hat, with the given information?

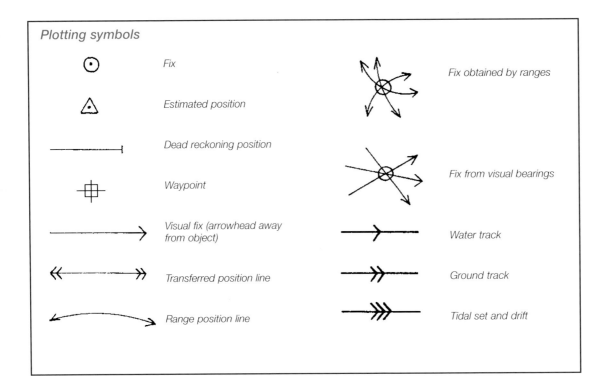

Plotting symbols

⊙	Fix
△	Estimated position
—————⊢	Dead reckoning position
⊕	Waypoint
————→	Visual fix (arrowhead away from object)
«————»»	Transferred position line
↙⌒→	Range position line
	Fix obtained by ranges
	Fix from visual bearings
—→—	Water track
—»»—	Ground track
—»»»—	Tidal set and drift

4.1

a) What do the rules say about the 'Right-of Way' of vessels at sea?

b) What do the rules say about keeping a look-out?

c) If you are in a situation where a risk of collision exists and you are required to give way to the other vessel, at what stage should you take avoiding action?

d) When taking action to avoid a collision at night, how can you help to ensure that the manoeuvre you make is immediately obvious to the other vessel?

4.2

In the following situations a risk of collision exists. Which is the give-way vessel and what action should be taken?

a)
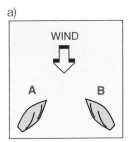

b)
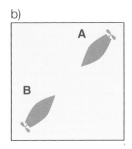

c)
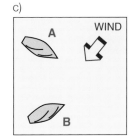

d)
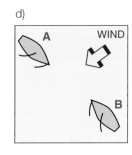

e)
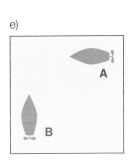

f)
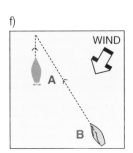

g)
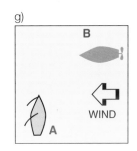

h)
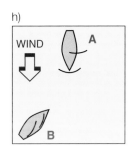

4.3

How can you tell if a risk of collision exists when in sight of an approaching vessel?

4.4

What are the meanings of the following day shapes?

a)   b)   c)   d)   e)   f)   g)

4.5

a) Give 4 situations when a sailing vessel on starboard tack would be the give-way vessel.

b) List 5 factors to be considered when determining a safe speed.

c) When crossing a Traffic Separation Scheme, should your heading or ground track be at right angles to the traffic flow?

4.6

At dusk, the skipper of a sailing yacht switches on the masthead tricolour, steaming light and pulpit lights to make the boat as visible as possible. Is this permitted by the rules?

4.7

What type of vessel is indicated by the following group of lights?

Give sizes, whether underway/making way, and aspect, i.e. port, starboard, from ahead or astern.

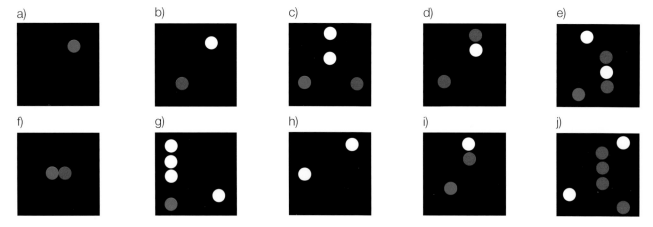

a) b) c) d) e)

f) g) h) i) j)

4.8

What are the meanings of the following sound signals?

a) — b) ▪ ▪ ▪ c) — — d) ▪ e) — ▪ ▪

f) ▪ ▪ g) — ▪ ▪ ▪ h) — — ▪ i) Bell for 5 seconds j) ▪ ▪ ▪ ▪ ▪ ▪

4.9

Use a diagram to illustrate the correct lights for:

a) A 20 knot, 10 metre powerboat from ahead.

b) A yacht fitted with tricolour, steaming light, sidelights and stern lights when motor sailing, viewed from the starboard side.

4.10

You see a vessel displaying a blue and white swallow-tailed flag.

What does this signify and what action should you take?

4.11

A risk of collision is developing between the vessels below, while at sea.

What action should the yacht take in order to ensure that a collision does not happen?

5.1

Fires are rare accidents on boats but skippers and crews must be aware of the hazards of fire at sea.

Suggest 4 of the most common causes.

5.2

a) What is the best way of avoiding a build-up of gas in the bilges?

b) Should a gas build-up be detected, what is the best of clearing it?

5.3

Which type of pyrotechnics are recommended for:

a) Signalling distress when 10 miles offshore, day or night?

b) Warning another vessel that there is a risk of collision?

c) Pinpointing position in a distress situation, day or night, within 3 miles of a rescuer?

d) Pinpointing position in a distress situation in bright daylight conditions to a helicopter?

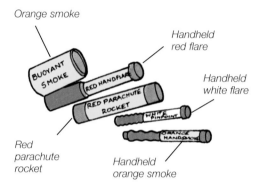

Orange smoke

Handheld red flare

Handheld white flare

Red parachute rocket

Handheld orange smoke

5.4

The yacht *Azure* is 2 miles south of Start Point lighthouse in position 50°11′.5N 004°38′.5W when a fire is detected. One crew member immediately uses the extinguisher while the other readies the liferaft.

The skipper prepares to send a mayday on the VHF-DSC radio which is inter-faced with GPS.

a) What action should be taken before the voice message is sent?

b) Write the voice message.

5.5

a) Suggest 3 important actions to take before throwing the liferaft over the side.

b) It is recommended that the largest, heaviest crew climb into the raft first. Why is this?

c) What are the priorities once all the crew are aboard the raft?

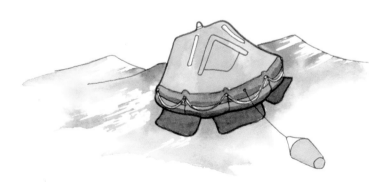

5.6

The crew of a vessel requiring assistance from a SAR helicopter need answers to the following questions:

a) The helmsman must steer on a very straight heading. At what angle to the wind should the boat steer?

b) The winchman is being lowered on a wire from the helicopter with the use of a hi-line.

How should the crew use the hi-line?

c) How have the crew prepared the boat?

d) Why should a red parachute rocket NOT be used when the helicopter is in the area?

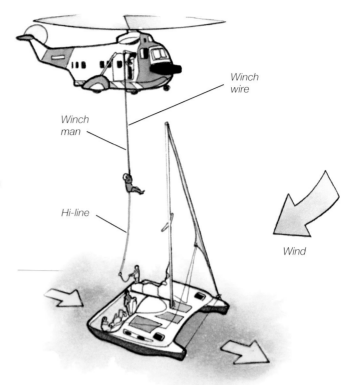

Winch wire

Winch man

Hi-line

Wind

5.7

a) What is a SART and what does it do?

b) What is an EPIRB and how is it used in distress situations?

c) An EPIRB must be registered with which organisation?

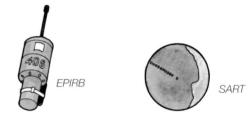

EPIRB

SART

5.8

a) What is the AVS (Angle of Vanishing Stability)?

b) What are the advantages if the AVS is high?

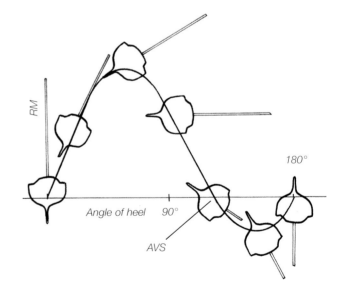

RM

180°

Angle of heel 90°

AVS

5.9

List 8 internationally recognised distress signals.

5.10

Coastguards regularly make Maritime Safety Information Broadcasts on VHF.

What information is included?

Use RYA Charts 1 & 2

6.1

How can a navigator tell at a glance if a charted buoy is lit?

6.2

What is the meaning of the following chart symbol?

6.3

Identify the unlit buoys at the following positions; describe the colour and characteristics of the lights that could be fitted to them.

    a)   50°16'.5N   004°28'.5W

    b)   50°16'.3N   004°33'.7W

6.4

Explain the following light characteristics:

    a)   Fl.G 2.5s

    b)   Oc.R.10s

    c)   Mo (U)

    d)   2 F.R. (vert). When is this type of light used?

6.5

Many buoys have white flashing lights. Suggest 3.

6.6

Use RYA Chart 2

    a)   Approaching Dartmouth at night the skipper is using the sectored light shown on the chart. If the boat is following the safe central sector describe the light that will be seen.

    b)   How will the skipper know if the boat is carried to the north by the tidal stream?

    c)   On which side of the boat should the green conical buoy be left?

6.7

What colour and light characteristics would the following buoys have?

a)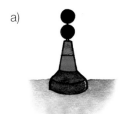 b)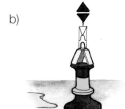 c) d)

6.8

a) What is this buoy? How is it used?

b) It can have various light characteristics, what are they?

6.9

a) You are heading south when you see a light on a buoy flashing nine times directly in front of you.
Which way should you turn (port or starboard) to stay to the safe side of the buoy?

b) While heading up a small river you come across a fork in the channel marked by a post painted red-green-red. Which is the preferred channel?

6.10

Use RYA Chart 1

a) The Eddystone lighthouse (SW of Plymouth) has two lights, what are their characteristics?

b) Would you expect to be able to see both lights from Plymouth Sound?

c) How high above the water is each light and from what level are they measured?

d) The nominal range of the flashing white light is shown on the chart as 20M. Explain why someone onboard a small craft would probably not be able to see it at this distance.

Use RYA Charts 1 & 2

7.1

Which of the following situations would you generally expect to give the roughest sea conditions?

    a)   Wind blowing with the direction of the tidal stream.

    b)   Wind blowing against the direction of the tidal stream.

7.2

When planning a passage, prudent navigators pay special attention to tidal gates.

Give a brief explanation of the term tidal gate.

7.3

Using tidal diamond ◁B▷ on RYA Chart 2, find the direction and rate of the tidal streams off Start Point.

    a)   HW Plymouth, springs?

    b)   4 hours before HW Plymouth, neaps?

    c)   2 hours after HW Plymouth, mid-range?

7.4

Using tidal diamond ◁G▷ on RYA Chart 2, find the direction and rate of the tidal stream four miles SE of South Coombe Island.

    a)   Friday 9th August between 1630 and 1730 BST?

    b)   Friday 5th July between 1524 and 1624 BST?

    c)   Thursday 13th June between 0400 and 0500 BST?

7.5

Use the tidal stream charts to answer the following:

    a)   What is the direction and rate of the tidal stream 5 miles north west of Alderney 1 hour before HW springs at Plymouth?

    b)   What is the direction and rate of the tidal stream about 10 miles north of Cherbourg on Saturday 25th May between 0700 and 0800 BST?

    c)   South of Salcombe, in the early morning of Monday 10th June, when does the tidal stream become west-going?

    d)   On Tuesday 23rd July a skipper is planning a passage from Falmouth towards Plymouth. When does the tidal stream turn to the east that morning?

7.6

On Monday 24th June a group of divers are planning a brief dive on a wreck site south of Jersey.

They need to dive when the tidal stream is as slack as possible. When is the best time to be underwater?

Use the tidal stream charts.

7.7

On Saturday 31st August a yacht skipper is planning a passage from St Peter Port in Guernsey to Cherbourg, via the Alderney Race. The wind is forecast to be SW 5.

The advice in the pilot book is to pass Banc de la Schole as the fair tide starts to make for the most favourable conditions.

Use the tidal stream charts to find the time of this tidal gate.

7.8

Using **RYA Chart 1** find the direction and rate of the tidal streams:

   a)   Between Alderney and Guernsey on Wednesday 31st January, between 0925 and 1125 UT.

        Use tidal diamond ⟨K⟩

   b)   West of Guernsey on Monday 1st July, between 0731 and 0831 BST.

        Use tidal diamond ⟨L⟩

   c)   North of Cap de la Hague on Saturday 16th March, between 0415 and 0545 UT.

        Use tidal diamond ⟨F⟩

Tidal heights 8

Use RYA Chart 2

8.1

a) The range of the tide = HW - ....

b) The height of tide = the amount of water above ....

c) The depth of water = charted depth + ...

d) A drying height is above chart datum and is coloured .... on Admiralty Charts (e.g. on RYA Charts 1 and 2).

e) The charted height (elevation) of a lighthouse or bridge is measured above ....

8.2

If the height of tide is 2.5m:

a) What is the depth of water at the charted sounding in position 50°18'.35N 004°28'.2W?

b) What is the depth of water in position 50°18'.6N 004°27'.6W?

8.3

a) Using the tidal levels information for Torquay on RYA Chart 2 what is the depth of water 0.2 miles south of the end of the breakwater at MLWS?

b) Using the tidal levels information for Holcombe Regis on RYA Chart 2 what is the depth of water at the drying height in the northern part of the bay at MLWN?

8.4

What are the times and heights of HW:

a) In the early morning of Wednesday 15th May at Plymouth?

b) On the evening of Saturday 31st August at St Helier?

c) On the morning of Thursday 1st August at St Malo?

8.5

What is the range of the tide at Plymouth:

a) During the midday period of Friday 5th July. Is it spring, neap or mid range?

b) During the early morning of Saturday 10th August. Is it spring, neap or mid range?

c) During the midday period of Thursday 9th May. Is it spring, neap or mid range?

8.6

a) What is the height of tide 2 hours before HW on the evening of Thursday 4th July at St Helier?

b) What is the height of tide 3$\frac{1}{2}$ hours after HW in the early morning of Saturday 24th August at Plymouth?

8.7

What will be the height of tide at Plymouth on Tuesday 4th June at 0630 BST?

8.8

On Wednesday 8th May at 1230 BST a yacht is preparing to anchor at Plymouth.

- a) What is the height of tide at 1230 BST?
- b) How much will the tide fall between 1230 BST and LW?
- c) The boat has a draught of 1.6m and the skipper wants to have a clearance of 1.0m at LW.

  What is the minimum depth of water to anchor in at 1230 BST?

8.9

At 2040 on Sunday 28th July a skipper picks up a mooring near St Helier for the night. The depth of water at 2040 BST is 6.5m and the boat has a draught of 1.5m.

Will this be safe? Calculate the clearance at LW.

8.10

Apply the secondary port differences to the following standard port tidal information.

Where required add 1 hour for BST.

a) **April**

	Time		Height	
	HW	LW	HW	LW
Standard port - Plymouth	0600	1300	5.5	0.8
Secondary port - Brixham	....	....	....	....
BST adjustment?	....	....	....	....
	____	____	____	____
	____	____	____	____

b) **June**

	Time		Height	
	HW	LW	HW	LW
Standard port – Saint Helier	1200	1730	9.5	2.7
Secondary port – Braye (Alderney)	....	....	....	....
BST adjustment?	....	....	....	....
	____	____	____	____
	____	____	____	____

c) **August**

	Time		Height	
	HW	LW	HW	LW
Standard port – Saint Malo	2206	0518	10.6	2.6
Secondary port – Carteret	....	....	....	....
BST adjustment?	....	....	....	....
	____	____	____	____
	____	____	____	____

8.11

Give the times and heights of HW and LW for the following:

- a) At Torquay, on the morning of Sunday 21st July.
- b) At Start Point, in the afternoon/evening of Tuesday 9th January.
- c) At Braye Harbour, in the afternoon/evening of Monday 13th May.

8.12

At 2000 BST on Monday 15th April the crew of a boat drawing 1.6m are preparing to anchor near Brixham.

What depth of water should they anchor in to ensure a clearance under the boat of 2.0m at the next LW?

8.13

On the morning of Sunday 30th June a vessel drawing 1.5m is departing Carteret.

Before she's able to clear the breakwater the crew hear a clunk, the engine stops and they drift alongside the West Jetty with a rope jammed around the propeller. As the depth of water alongside the Jetty at 0925 BST is 2.8m the vessel will ground later, enabling the crew to clear the propeller.

a) At what time will the boat ground?

b) Will she dry out completely?

c) When will she re-float?

Chartwork position 9

Use RYA Chart 1   Use variation 7°W   Use deviation card on page 123
All times are BST   All answers to be given in BST
Depths given are reduced to datum

9.1

The following is an extract from the logbook of a boat leaving Plymouth on passage towards Fowey. The entries begin as the boat passes the red buoy off Penlee Point.

Time	Co°(M)	Log	Wind	Leeway	Baro	Depth	Remarks
1015	250	0.0	NW3	nil	1008	11.2m	Leave Plymouth
1028	250	1.4	NW2	nil	1008	24.6m	South of Rame Head. Alter course to 280°(M)
1230	280	12.8	NW2	nil	1008	32.3m	DR. Position, approaching Fowey

Plot the DR position at 1230 BST.

9.2

At 0730 an angling boat is in position 50°10'.0N   005°20'.0W steering on a heading of 265°(M) at 8 knots. The tidal stream has been calculated as 030°(T) 2.0 knots.

a) Plot the EP at 0830 BST.

b) What is the speed over the ground? (SOG).

c) What is the course over the ground? (COG).

9.3

On Sunday 30th June a yacht is in position 50°12'.0N   004°54'.0W steering a heading of 310°(M).

At 1234 the log reading is 15.4.

a) What time is HW Plymouth? Is it springs or neaps?

b) What is the tidal stream between 1234 and 1334 BST at tidal diamond ⟨C⟩ ?

c) Plot the EP at 1334 BST when the log reading is 20.6.

d) During the hour what is the average speed through the water that the skipper would have seen on the log?

e) What is the SOG and COG?

9.4

The skipper of a motor cruiser on passage towards Plymouth has put the centre of the compass rose to the southwest of Plymouth into the GPS as a waypoint. At 1435 BST the direction and distance to the waypoint is given as 200°(T) 6.8 miles and the helmsman is steering on a heading of 085°(M) at 14 knots.

The skipper estimates that the boat will pass more than a mile north of the shallowest part of the Hand Deeps.

The tidal stream has been calculated as 135°(T) 1.0 knot.

a) Plot the projected EP for 1535 BST.

b) How close to the shallow area will the boat pass?

c) At about what time will the boat pass the yellow buoy marking the Hand Deeps?

9.5

At 1530 on Friday 9th August the skipper of a yacht leaving Cherbourg towards Plymouth is in position 49°47′.4N   004°49′.4W. The boat is on a heading of 325°(M) at 6.5 knots.

The skipper expects to be well clear of the restricted area marked on the chart *Diving Prohibited*.

    a)   What time is HW at Plymouth? Is it springs or neaps?

    b)   What will the tidal stream be between 1530 and 1630 BST? Use the tidal stream charts.

    c)   Plot the EP at 1630 BST. How far outside the restricted area will the boat pass?

    d)   Will the safe water mark CH1 pass on the port side or starboard side of the boat?

9.6

A yacht on a night passage to Saint Peter Port is south of Guernsey, tacking into a northerly breeze.

Draw a waypoint web from a waypoint 1.0 mile due east of Saint Martin's Point in order to be able to quickly plot the vessel's position while underway.

What colour light will be visible from Saint Martin's Point lighthouse when the GPS display shows the bearing and distance to the waypoint to be 030°(T) 4.5 miles?

9.7

Using the following extract from a vessel's logbook, plot the EP at 1525 BST.

Date	Time	Log	Co°(M)	Wind	Leeway	Baro	Depth	Remarks
Sunday	1425	13.2	290	SE 4	nil	1010	32.0m	Position: 49°38′.0N 005°18′.4W
April 28th	1500	17.0	290	SE 4	nil	1010	8.8m	Depth rapidly shoaling
	1525	20.4	290	SE 4	nil	1010	22.0m	

Use tidal diamond ◁K▷.   Comment on the reason for the rapidly shoaling depth at 1500 BST.

9.8

At 1210 the skipper of a motorboat fixes position while south west of Alderney:

    Water tower at Saint Anne in transit with Chimney (85) near the airport (047°(M).

    Casquets lighthouse bearing 303°(M).

    30 metre contour line.

Using the following extract from the motorboat's logbook, plot the EP at 1240 BST.

Date	Time	Log	Co°(C)	Wind	Leeway	Baro	Depth	Remarks
Monday	1210	5.6	140	N 2	nil	1016	30m	Fix as above.
13th May	1240	11.6	140	N 2	nil	1016	36m	

Use the tidal stream charts.

What were the vessel's SOG and COG?

9.9

At 0700 BST on Monday 1st July a motorboat, on route to Falmouth is entering the Traffic Separation Scheme off the Casquets; GPS position: 49°50'.0N   005°40'.0W.

In order to cross the traffic flow at right angles the helmsman is asked to hold a course of 345°(C). Use the deviation card on page 123.

If a boat speed of 12.0 knots is maintained:

a)   Estimate where will the vessel exit the TSS (far edge of the purple boundary)

b)   What will be the vessel's SOG and COG during the crossing?

c)   How long will it take for the vessel to reach the exit point?

Use tidal diamond ◇H◇.

9.10

On Tuesday 16th April a yacht is sailing to windward in a fresh northerly breeze.

At 1620 BST while on port tack the skipper plots the GPS position: 49°29'.6N   005°28'.2W.

The yacht's best courses to windward are: Port tack 045°(C). Starboard tack 315°(C).

The skipper plans to tack in ¹/₂ hour, aiming to clear the overfalls to the north east of Sark.

Plot the COG for each tack to see if it's likely that the boat will clear the overfalls.

Use tidal diamond ◇N◇.   Leeway 5°.   Boat speed 7.0 knots.

9.11

On Tuesday 30th April a powerboat, approximately one mile south of the Traffic Separation Scheme is heading towards the northeast, running parallel to the TSS.

At 1115 BST, log reading 44 miles, the skipper fixes position using three radar ranges:

Platte Fougere Racon (P)   10.7M

Casquets Racon (T)   8.2M

Channel West Racon (O)   8.9M

Plot the fix.

9.12

After plotting the radar fix from question 9.11 the skipper adjusts the autopilot to steer a course of 065°(C) towards a waypoint at position: 49°52'.6 N   005°30'.2W. The vessel's boat speed is 12.0 knots.

a)   Plot a XTE ladder from the waypoint to the fix to enable the boat's position to be quickly plotted.

b)   If the course of 065°(C) is maintained without adjustment for tidal set and drift, which of the following XTE readings would the GPS display after 1/2 hour, when the log reads 50 miles?   Use tidal diamond ◇H◇.

  i)   XTE zero.

  ii)   XTE 0.5M to starboard, steer left.

  iii)   XTE 1.2M to port, steer right.

c)   Assuming the current COG and SOG are maintained, what will the bearing and distance to the waypoint be at 1215 BST?

d)   With regard to hazards on route, comment on the advisability of the skipper's decision not to alter course in order to stay close to the original rhumb line.

Course to steer

Use RYA Chart 1   Use variation 7°W
All times are BST   All answers to be given in BST

10.1

An angling boat has been fishing off Lizard Point west of Falmouth. It is returning to Falmouth making for the East Cardinal Buoy off the Manacles Rocks at a speed of 8 knots.

a) What is the distance from its position at 49°56'.0N 006°04'.0W to the buoy?

b) What is the magnetic course to steer to allow for a tidal stream of 065°(T) at 2.0 knots?

c) Will it take just over an hour or less than an hour to get to the buoy?

d) When the buoy is first sighted will it be dead ahead, or on the port or starboard bow?

10.2

At 1635 a motor cruiser on passage down the channel at a cruising speed of 25 knots is south of Salcombe in position: 50°10'.0N 004°46'.5W making for a position 5 miles south of the Eddystone Rocks lighthouse. What is the magnetic course to steer to allow for the tidal stream of 325°(T) at 1.8 knots?

10.3

On Sunday 4th August a yacht is returning from Alderney to Plymouth making for the yellow buoy in the harbour entrance. At 0547 BST the GPS gives the position as: 50°12'.2N 005°09'.8W.

a) What time is HW Plymouth? Is it springs or neaps?

b) What will be the tidal stream between 0547 and 0647 BST at tidal diamond ⟨C⟩?

c) What is the magnetic course to steer if the boat speed is 6.0 knots?

d) "Shall I just aim for it?", asks the helmsman when the buoy is sighted. Is this a good idea?

10.4

On Monday 27th May a yacht on passage towards Cherbourg is using the centre of the compass rose off Cherbourg as a waypoint for plotting positions. At 1317 BST the distance and direction to the waypoint is given as 247°(T) 2.4M.

a) What will be the tidal stream between 1317 and 1417, and 1417 and 1517 BST, using the tidal stream charts?

b) What is the magnetic course to steer to the western end of the breakwater if the boat speed is 6.5 knots?

c) If the skipper estimates that the westerly wind will give 5° leeway what course should be steered instead?

10.5

On Friday 17th May a powerboat, bound for Cherbourg is closing the coast at a boat speed of 15.0 knots.

At 1920 BST the skipper plots position with reference to a waypoint at the centre of the compass rose north of Cherbourg 045°(T) 6.0M.

a) What is the compass course to steer, SOG and COG to a waypoint at the safewater buoy: 49°49'.6N 004°52'.0W?

b) Would you expect the bearing to the Safe Water buoy displayed by the GPS to remain fairly constant during the trip?

   Use tidal diamond ⟨J⟩. Use deviation card on page 123.

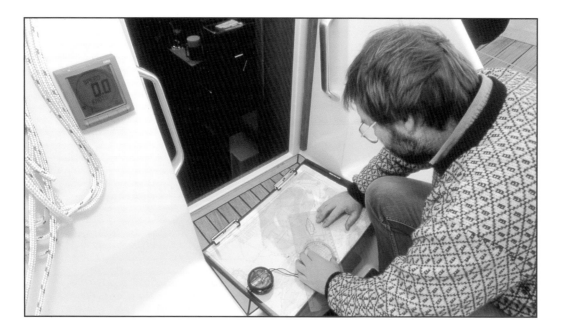

10.6

At 2100 BST on Wednesday 22nd May the mate of a vessel departing Alderney fixes position:

Braye Harbour leading lights in transit.

Gros du Raz light (off Cap de la Hague): 109°(M).

50 metre contour line.

What is the compass course to steer and ETA to a waypoint off the Cherbourg peninsula: 49°53'.0N 005°00'.0W?

Boat speed 12.0 knots. Use the tidal stream charts.

10.7

On Saturday 1st June a powerboat making 18.0 knots is south of the Alderney Race, heading for the French coast. At 1900 BST the vessel's position is plotted with reference to the nearest compass rose 180°(T) 7.2M.

    a)   What is the compass course to steer, SOG and COG to a waypoint off Dielette: 49°40'.0N 005°02'.0W?

    b)   As they close the coast and enter shallower water the skipper expects the tidal stream to become lighter than indicated by the tidal stream charts.

        How would any tidal fluctuations show up on the GPS display with regard to:

        i)   XTE.

        ii)   Bearing to Waypoint.

        iii)   SOG.

Use the tidal stream charts.

10.8

On Wednesday 24th January a yacht bound for Falmouth is sailing at 6.0 knots in a strong northerly breeze.

At 2125 UT, the skipper plots position: 50°02'.8N 005°40'.0W.

    a)   What is the compass course to steer and ETA to a waypoint ¹/₂ mile due south of the Saint Anthony Head lighthouse?

        Use tidal diamond ⟨E⟩.   Leeway 10°.

    b)   How would you expect the XTE and Bearing to Waypoint displayed by the GPS to react if the leeway proved to be greater than originally estimated?

Electronic navigation aids 11

11.1

A basic through-hull log supplies which of the following types of information?

a) Speed over the ground.

b) Speed through the water.

c) Both.

11.2

The through-hull impeller log is a popular choice for pleasure boats.

Give two other examples of logs that might be found supplying speed information on small craft.

11.3

Which is potentially more dangerous, a log which over reads or one that under reads? Give reasons.

11.4

Which of the following is true with regard to depth sounders commonly found on boats?

a) They display the depth of water, from the surface to the seabed.

b) They display the amount of water under the keel of the boat.

c) They can normally be calibrated to show either.

11.5

How might a depth sounder be affected by the turbulence caused from the wash of a passing ship?

11.6

A Global Positioning System (GPS) receiver displays position very precisely.

How accurate are these positions likely to be?

a) Within 95 metres 15% of the time.

b) Within 1 metre 100% of the time.

c) Within 15 metres 95% of the time.

11.7

Use this GPS display to answer the following questions.

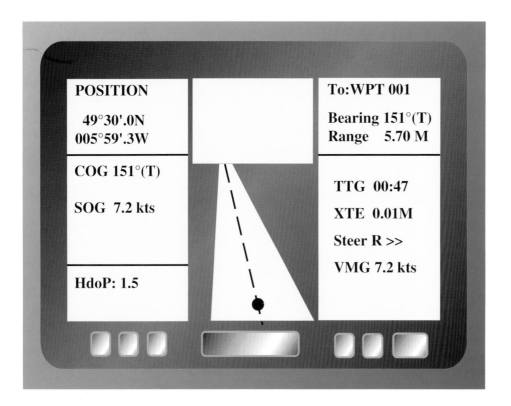

a) Waypoint 001 is at the centre of the compass rose south west of Guernsey (RYA Chart 1).

   Would you expect the bearing and range to the waypoint, to give the same position on the chart as the latitude and longitude? If so, would there be any practical advantage of using one method of plotting over the other?

b) If the time now were 1113 when would you estimate arriving at the waypoint?

c) The cross track error (XTE) displayed in this example is very small (0.01M).

   In which of the following examples might it be acceptable for XTE to be quite large?

   i) Piloting through the Little Russel.

   ii) On a channel crossing when cross-tides cancel each other out.

d) If the cross track error started to increase how would you expect the central display to change?

e) Other instruments onboard show a speed through the water of 6.0 knots and a course of 177°(M).

   Which of the following tidal set and drifts is likely to be affecting the boat?

   i) 100°(T) 2.5 knots

   ii) 310°(T) 3.5 knots

f) What does the HdoP 1.5 displayed in the bottom left-hand corner of the screen mean?

g) In this example, the display shows the speed over ground (SOG) and velocity made good (VMG) to be the same (7.2 knots). Would this be the case if the vessel were a yacht, tacking toward the waypoint?

11.8

The GPS system has proved to be generally reliable and very accurate, however good practice at sea doesn't rely on just one source of information.

List three other sources of navigational information that could be used to back up the GPS.

11.9

Listed below are some characteristics that apply to electronic charts.

Which type of chart does each characteristic apply to? i) Raster ii) Vector

   a)   The charts are scanned versions of the paper equivalent.

   b)   Information on the chart is grouped and held in databases or layers.

   c)   The charts should not be magnified beyond the scale at which they were produced.

   d)   The level of detail on the chart changes when zooming in or out.

   e)   The charts can be interrogated to reveal extra information about a selected feature.

   f)   The charts can be magnified beyond the scale at which they were produced.

11.10

Explain why it might be dangerous to navigate using an electronic chart that has been magnified beyond the scale at which it was originally produced.

11.11

   a)   When using radar for a fix, why is it likely that range will give a more reliable position than bearing?

   b)   Why might it be difficult to locate a narrow harbour entrance using radar?

   c)   While monitoring the radar you notice that a target has remained on a steady bearing while progressing towards the centre of the screen. What should this alert you to?

Pilotage 12

Use RYA Charts 1 and 2

12.1

Busy harbours and ports are increasingly making use of traffic signals to control vessel movements.

Match the following meanings to the International Port Traffic Signals below:

a) Vessels may proceed. Two way traffic.

b) A vessel may proceed when she has received specific orders to do so, except that vessels which navigate outside the main channel need not comply with the main message.

c) Serious emergency. All vessels to stop or divert according to instructions.

12.2

The skipper of a vessel departing Gorey (east coast of Jersey) at night, is using the leading lights as a back transit in order to stay clear of the off-lying rocks. As the tidal stream begins to affect the boat the skipper notices that the lights are no longer in line, but look as follows:

a) Which way must the helmsman steer (port or starboard) to bring the lights back into transit?

b) Once back in transit, what colour will the forward light show?

12.3

A motorboat on a night passage from Dartmouth to Salcombe is approaching the overfalls off Start Point.

a) How could the skipper use the Skerries Point lighthouse to avoid passing through the charted overfalls?

b) What will the bearing to Start Point lighthouse be when the boat has passed to the west of the hazard?

12.4

Use the notes in the extracts to answer the following pilotage questions:

a) When visiting Fowey, how can you identify the moorings that have been set-aside for visitors?

b) Is it advisable for vessels visiting Looe to take the passage between Looe Island and the mainland?

c) At what state of tide would you expect the lock gates of Plymouth's Sutton Harbour Marina to stay open?

d) What should you beware of when anchoring to the west of Brixham Harbour?

e) Why might it be difficult to discern the lights marking Torquay Harbour and Marina at night?

f) How long would you expect a boat drawing 1.5 metres to remain afloat at neap tide, while alongside the West Jetty at Carteret?

g) What conspicuous object, just under a mile NNW of the entrance to Porbail, could help to identify the harbour by day?

h) How is depth of water over the sill displayed at Granville's Port de Merel marina, and what problem might be encountered when trying to read the display on a fine day?

12.5

On Sunday 3rd March, a group of sea anglers from Kingswear are enjoying some early season fishing along the Skerries Bank (50°14'.2N 004°36'.2W). During the afternoon the visibility starts to decrease until at 1520 UT they are enveloped in thick fog.

How could the anglers make use of their depth sounder to help them pilot the boat safely back to the entrance of the River Dart?

12.6

At 1135 BST on Saturday 31st August you are approaching Salcombe in a fresh southerly breeze.

Before closing the coast you prudently heave-to in deep water to survey the entrance through binoculars, but find it difficult to make out the sea conditions inshore due to a heavy swell.

a) Is it likely that you will be able to safely enter Salcombe?

b) Where could advice about conditions in the entrance be reliably obtained?

12.7

The crew of a vessel approaching Falmouth from the south at night, have just identified Saint Anthony Head light which is occulting white every 15 seconds. A few moments later they are surprised to see an easterly cardinal pass close down the starboard side of the boat.

The skipper decides to call the Coastguard to report that the Manacle's east cardinal buoy has drifted out of position. Is the skipper's information likely to be correct?

12.8

On Friday 5th July a yacht, draft 1.6m, is sailing north towards the River Yealm in an easterly breeze.

The skipper has worked out the ETA at Wembury Bay to be 1200 BST and has asked you to find answers to the following pilotage questions enabling the vessel to be navigated into the river.

a) At 1200 BST in which direction will the tidal stream be flowing near the coast, roughly east or west?

b) How can the Western and Eastern Ebb rocks be avoided when approaching Wembury Bay?

c) Once in the bay, how will you know when to turn toward the river, and what pilotage aid is available ashore to keep the vessel clear of Mouthstone Ledge?

d) What marks the end of the sand bar at the river entrance?

e) Having passed the sand bar, when is it advisable to turn northeast towards the north shore and what navigation mark should be ahead?

f) At the moment the plan is to pay just a short visit to the river, departing for Plymouth at 1600 BST. Is this plan likely to be achievable?

g) If required, is it possible to sail into the river today?

13.1

Which of the following wind circulations indicate low pressure in the Northern Hemisphere?

a)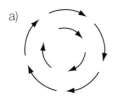
b)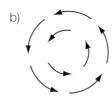

13.2

A skipper and crew are in harbour making the final preparations to a boat they've chartered for a weekend cross-channel cruise. Before departing they receive a weather bulletin forecasting that a vigorous depression will be passing through their sea area soon.

Which of the following actions should they take?

a) Quickly complete the preparations in order to depart as soon as possible in the hope that they can make it across before the weather gets too bad.

b) Take a little more time with the preparations to ensure that the vessel is ready for rough weather, then set out.

c) Delay departure until the depression has passed, and the weather improves. If necessary changing their plan for a cross-channel passage in favour of more local ports.

13.3

What Beaufort wind force would you associate with the following conditions in the open sea?

a) Moderate waves, many white crests.

b) Sea heaps up, spray, breaking waves, foam blows in streaks.

13.4

What are the meanings of the following terms?

a) Imminent
b) Veering
c) Good
d) Severe gale (Force 9)
e) Fair
f) Later
g) Fog

13.5

You are running before a brisk westerly breeze on the edge of a shallow depression in the Northern Hemisphere.

According to Buy Ballot's Law, is the low to the north or the south of you?

13.6

What wind direction and strength, (light, moderate or strong) would you expect from the synopsises below:

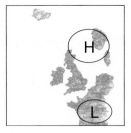

a) In the Thames Estuary:
High Viking.
Low central France.

b) In the Irish Sea:
Deepening low
Shannon.

c) In the English Channel:
High central France.

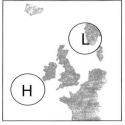

d) In the Western Isles
of Scotland:
Low North Utsire
High Sole.

e) In the English Channel:
High central Scotland.

f) Along the East Coast:
Low (filling) German
Bight.

13.7

Under what conditions are the following most likely to occur?

a) Land (radiation) fog.

b) Sea (advection) fog.

13.8

Use the synoptic chart on page 41.

a) Which sea area could be described as having cyclonic weather conditions?

b) Describe the weather in the English Channel, include: cloud, precipitation, wind strength and direction.

c) What type of weather front is passing through sea areas: Forties, Dogger, Humber and Thames?

d) Where would you expect, bright and breezy conditions with blustery showers, England or Ireland?

e) In which sea area are the stronger winds, Viking or Biscay?

13.9

It's 0700 on a fine summer morning, with clear skies and light winds. The weather forecast has indicated that a sea breeze is likely during the day.

Give a brief description of where and when you would expect the breeze to blow and how this breeze might change during the evening.

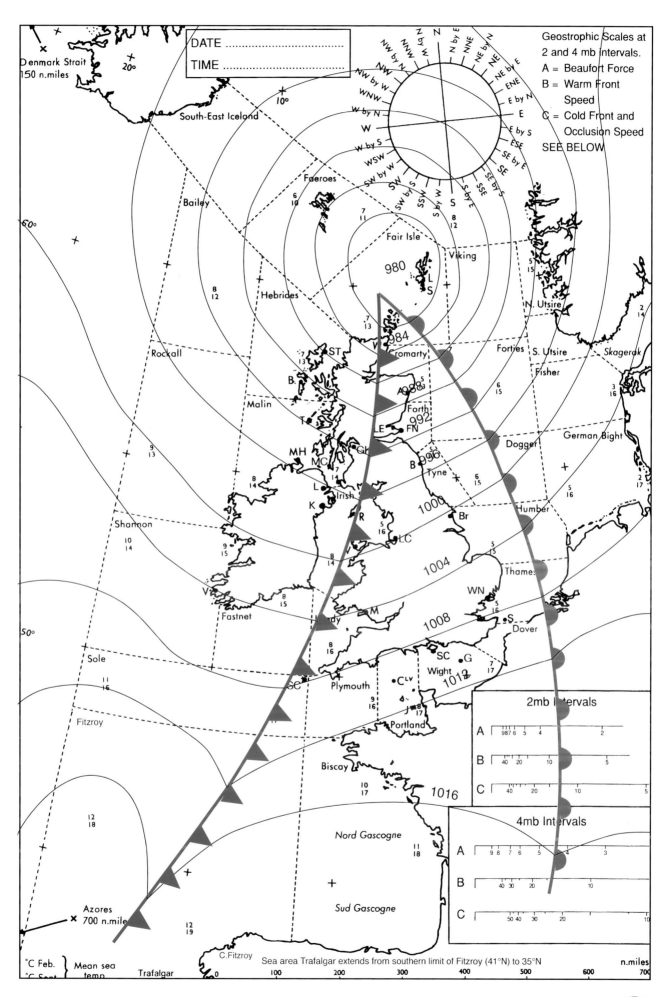

Passage planning

Use RYA Charts 1 and 2

Passage planning doesn't always result in definitive answers, sometimes there is more than one option.

14.1

At 1620 BST on Friday 21st June a yacht, bound for Dartmouth is at the South Cardinal buoy off Mill Head (North Coombe Island).

With a northwesterly breeze, a beat is in prospect and the skipper needs to decide which is the best tack to set off on. Close hauled, the yacht will sail 045° off the wind at 5.0 knots.

Using diamond ◇D◇ for tidal information, decide which tack would be most advantageous.

14.2

On Sunday 25th August, you and two friends are on board an 11m yacht in Plymouth, planning a cruise around the Channel Islands and French coast.

It's decided that you would like to visit Braye Harbour on Alderney, Saint Helier on Jersey and Saint Malo in France, before returning to Plymouth, (perhaps via Cherbourg).

The weather forecast for the next five days is as follows:

Monday	NE	4-5
Tuesday	E	3
Wednesday	S	7 occasionally gale 8
Thursday	SW	4-5
Friday	NW	5

i)   In what order would you visit these harbours?

ii) Would returning to Plymouth via Cherbourg be a good plan for Friday?

14.3

On Saturday 1st June the crew of a dive boat are returning from a dive near Le Chats West Cardinal when they hear a radio message from a vessel at position: 49°23'.0N 005°37'.0W requesting a tow due to engine failure.

On arrival at the scene at 1900 BST, a line is passed and they start towing the stricken craft into port.

If the maximum speed achievable while towing is 5.0 knots, which harbour should they make for Saint Peter Port or Saint Helier?

Use the tidal stream charts from the extracts to help you make your decision.

14.4

At 2030 BST on Sunday 12th May a yacht, drawing 1.7m is departing Torquay, bound for Salcombe.

The weather forecast is: NW3, Fair, Good.

Prepare a passage plan for the journey; the plan should include the following:

i)   Overall distance.

ii)   Passage time (boat speed 5.0 knots).

iii) ETA at Salcombe.

iv)   Clearance over the bar at the entrance to Salcombe, on arrival.

v)   Dangers/Obstructions en route.

vi) The plan should also incorporate the following waypoints, forming a route. The waypoints have been placed in positions, which are convenient for checking by traditional navigation while underway, using depth contours and lights.

Plot the waypoints, then check the traditional 'back up' navigation.

Departure

1.	50°27'.0N 004°31'.5W	On the 10m contour, south of Torquay.
2.	50°23'.95N 004°28'.1W	Due east of Berry Head light, on the 30m contour.
3.	50°20'.65N 004°29'.8W	The Bull red buoy in transit with N Hurleston Cardinal Buoy, depth increasing off the 30m contour.
4.	50°17'.7N 004°31'.4W	Dartmouth's isophase directional lights turning from white to red, 30m contour.
5.	50°14'.1N 004°34'.0W	Start Point fixed red light disappearing from view, 50m contour.
6.	50°12'.0N 004°37'.0W	Start Point light bearing 330°(M).
7.	50°11'.25N 004°46'.4W	Salcombe's directional lights turning from green to white, Start Point light disappearing from view.

Destination

50°12'.8N 004°46'.5W	White sector of Salcombe's directional light dead ahead, 10m contour.

Once the waypoints are plotted, record the bearing and distance for each leg of the route.

14.5

At 1115 BST on Saturday 27th July the skippers of two different vessels are discussing their proposed departure times for a passage from Braye Harbour to Cherbourg.

One of them, the skipper of a 10m planing hull power boat (cruising speed 20 knots in smooth water) has decided to leave within the hour.

The other, who sails a 10m yacht intends to wait until a little after 1400 BST.

Are the skippers' departure times correct, and if so, why do they differ?

The weather forecast is: E 4 Fair, Good.

14.6

The SOLAS V Regulations require that passage plans are made and that a number of key points are taken into account.

Give a brief summary of what should be included in a passage plan with regard to the following:

i) Weather.

ii) Tides.

iii) The vessel.

iv) The crew.

v) Navigational dangers.

vi) Contingency plans.

vii) Contacts ashore.

Passage making 15

Use RYA Charts 1 and 2
Use variation 7°W on Chart 1 and 6°W on Chart 2
All times in BST   All answers to be given in BST

On Monday 3rd June you intend to make a daylight passage from Salcombe to Torquay as skipper onboard your 10m yacht which has an average cruising speed of 6.0 knots.

The forecast is for moderate to fresh westerly winds and good visibility.

15.1 Salcombe to Torquay

a) What time is HW Plymouth? Is it a spring or neap range?

b) HW Salcombe is 0747 BST 5.2m LW 0.5m.

   Between what times is it possible to cross the bar at Salcombe?

c) What is the approximate passage time?

d) Between what times are the tidal streams favourable?

e) Are there any access problems at Torquay?

f) Does the weather forecast indicate this is going to be a pleasant passage and a sheltered port of arrival?

g) Are there any hazards for the passage?

15.2 Salcombe to Torquay

When will you leave? Give reasons.

15.3 Salcombe to Torquay

You plan to use the GPS to check positions on route. The following waypoints are put into the GPS:

1. The centre of the compass rose south of South Coombe Island.

2. Position 50°25'.0N 004°25'.0W.

3. The seaward end of the breakwater at Torquay.

At 0808 BST the direction and distance to the compass rose waypoint is given as 096°(T) 9.8 miles.   Plot the fix.

15.4 Salcombe to Torquay

From the 0808 BST fix you ask the helmsman to steer 100°(M) while a course to steer is calculated to allow for a tidal stream of 060°(T) 1.5 knots. The plan is to sail about 1.5 miles south of Start Point lighthouse to avoid the rough water. Suddenly you are called on deck to deal with a problem with the rigging. While this is being done the boat speed falls to 3.5 knots.

If the heading is maintained will the boat clear the overfalls?

Plot a projected EP for 0908 BST of find out.

15.5 Salcombe to Torquay

At 0910 BST the GPS gives the direction and distance to the compass rose waypoint as 111°(T) 4.5 miles.

a) What is the magnetic course to steer from this position to the Bull red buoy east of Dartmouth?

The boat speed is now 6.5 knots. Use the tidal stream charts.

b) You estimate that the westerly wind will cause 10° leeway.

How will the course to steer to the Bull buoy need to be adjusted to compensate for the wind?

c) At approximately what time will the boat reach the buoy?

d) When the buoy is sighted will it be dead ahead, on the port bow or on the starboard bow?

How can you check that the course is correct?

15.6 Salcombe to Torquay

At 1040 BST the range and bearing to the second waypoint is displayed as 033°(T) range 2.3M. Plot the fix. After this position is plotted, the GPS display is changed to show the distance and direction to the waypoint on Torquay breakwater.

"Shall I just steer that course?" asks the helmsman. What should the answer be?

15.7 Salcombe to Torquay

You expect to arrive at the marina at 1130 BST. HW Torquay is at 0821 BST 4.8m LW 0.5m

a) What will be the height of tide at 1130 BST at Torquay?

b) On the plan of the marina what is the least depth of water shown by the pontoon berths?

c) What depth of water will there be on the berths at 1130 BST, and at the next LW?

At lunchtime on Monday 13th May the skipper of a yacht, draft 1.5 metres, is preparing a passage plan from Carteret to Plymouth.

Weather forecast: NE 3-4. Backing N 5 for a time. Fair. Good.

The skipper is eager to depart soon, in order to make as much progress as possible before the wind becomes northerly.

15.8 Carteret to Plymouth

a) What is the earliest time that afternoon that the boat can leave the non-tidal marina at Carteret?

b) Is this a suitable time to set off in order to have a favourable tidal stream towards the north?

c) If possible the skipper would like to pass through the Alderney Race with a favourable, but light tidal stream, in order to avoid the rough sea conditions associated with wind against tide in the area. Is this achievable if the wind stays NE for the next 4 or 5 hours? The yacht will sail to windward approximately 045° off the wind at a boat speed of 6.0 knots.

d) In order to keep track of the vessel's progress relative to the race, the skipper has entered the following waypoints into the GPS:

WTP 001: 49°28'.6N   005°02'.0W

WTP 002: 49°35'.2N   005°06'.0W

WTP 003: 49°41'.8N   005°10'.1W

WTP 004: 49°48'.2N   005°14'.0W

What are the ideal target times for the yacht to reach these waypoints in order to have the best chance of passing through the race with the lightest favourable tidal stream?

15.9 Carteret to Plymouth

At 1740 BST the yacht is 3¹/₂ miles west of Cap de Flamanville, when a crew member comes on deck to report flooding in the heads. While the skipper goes with the crew to investigate, the mate is asked to check the nearest available port for access.

Is the marina at Diellette likely to be accessible?

15.10 Carteret to Plymouth

Having quickly discovered and fixed the heads problem the skipper settles the crew down, makes some tea, then plots the boat's 1800 BST position with reference to waypoint 004: 335°(T) 7.2M.

   a) Plot the position.

   b) Does the 1800 position indicate that they are likely to reach waypoint 004 at the planned time?

15.11 Carteret to Plymouth

With the race successfully negotiated the vessel's position at 2010 BST is:
49°53'.2 N   005°13'.6W.

At about this time the wind backs, as forecast, to the north. Force 4-5.

Which tack should the skipper set off on in order to make the best progress towards Plymouth?

15.12 Carteret to Plymouth

   a) At 2230 BST the skipper plots position with reference to a waypoint at the centre of the compass rose to the north of Cherbourg: 100°(T) 9.0M. Plot the position.

   b) During the past hour or so the crew have been kept busy watching out for ships due to heavy traffic in the area. When viewed from the 2230 position, which way are the ships north of the boat heading?

      i) Generally in an easterly direction.

      ii) Generally in a westerly direction.

Explain the reason for your answer.

15.13 Carteret to Plymouth

Around midnight the wind starts to veer and by 0030 BST, with the yacht in position:

50°09'.0N   005°00'.W the crew are enjoying a reach with the breeze blowing from the northeast again.

   a) Plot the compass course to steer to the Fl.Y.2s buoy off Penlee Point at the entrance to Plymouth.

   b) What is the SOG and COG to the buoy?

   c) How long should it take to reach the buoy?

      Boat speed 6.0 knots.   Leeway 5°   Use tidal diamond ⟨C⟩

Answers

1.1

a) The yacht is on port tack because the wind is coming over the port side.

b) The green buoy is on the leeward bow.

c) F.

d) The red buoy is on the port bow.

e) C.

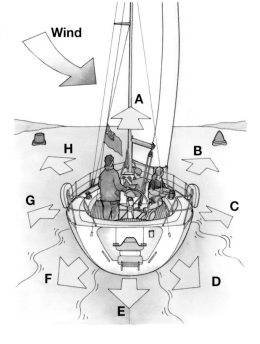

1.2

a) Bowline.

b) A bowline makes a non-slip loop in the end of a rope. It has many uses, including mooring to rings or cleats and attaching jib sheets.

1.3

a) A - Delta.

B - Danforth.

C - CQR or Plough.

D - Fisherman's or Admiralty Pattern.

E - Bruce.

b) The Fisherman's or Admiralty Pattern anchor has poor holding in mud or sand but good in weedy or rocky areas.

1.4

a) 4 x the maximum depth = 16m.

b) 6 x the maximum depth = 24m.

c) Nylon is best for anchor warps, and mooring warps too; because it has some stretch.

d) It is important to show an anchor ball to comply with the International Regulations for the Prevention of Collisions at Sea. If a vessel fails to show the signal while at anchor and another boat hits it, the anchored vessel would be deemed to be partly responsible.

e) An anchor light should be shown in the forepart of the vessel. This is an all round white light.

1.5

Any 4 from:

Shelter from the wind and swell at the time of anchoring.

Shelter from any forecast weather change.

Sufficient depth of water at low water.

Room for the boat to swing round when the tide turns or the wind changes.

Clear of moorings and other obstructions.

Out of a channel and away from a leading line used by other vessels.

In an area of good holding ground like mud or sand.

1.6

a)   A rolling hitch will take the weight off another rope (red in the diagram) temporarily to relieve the strain if there is a problem, for example, a riding turn on a winch.

b)   The blue rope will not slide to the right but will lock because of the two turns on that side.

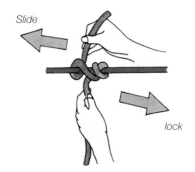

Chart familiarisation 2

2.1

a) Longitude   b) Latitude

2.2

i)	C	ii)	D	iii)	F
iv)	A	v)	H	vi)	K
vii)	G	viii)	B		

2.3

a) 60 minutes   b) 1 sea mile   c) knot

2.4

a) Wreck, depth unknown, which is considered dangerous to surface navigation.

b) Limit of restricted area.

c) Rock awash at chart datum.

d) Major light or lighthouse.

e) Overfalls, rip tides or races.

f) Wreck with a depth of 20 metres, obtained by soundings.

2.5

a) Rock which covers and uncovers.

b) Recommended anchorage.

c) Tidal diamond E.

d) Oil production platform.

e) Drying height of 1.1 metres above chart datum.

f) Boarding place for pilots.

2.6

a) 306°(T)   3.1 miles.

b) 040°(T)   2.25 miles.

c) 155°(T)   1.6 miles.

d) 258°(T)   5.7 miles.

2.7

a) Chimney.

b) Charted depth of 7.8 metres.

c) Sh. M. The nature of the seabed is shells and mud in this area.

d) Wreck, swept by wire, with a depth of 38 metres.

2.8

The *Admiralty list of Symbols and Abbreviations* is published as chart No. 5011, even though it has been in book form for many years.

Compass & position fixing

3.1

Variation was 7°30'W in 1997 decreasing 6' annually. So 6°48'W in 2004.

This is always rounded to the nearest degree.

3.2

 a) 236°(M)

 b) 057°(M)

3.3

 a) 133°(T)

 b) 341°(T)

3.4

 a) Deviation is the effect of the boat's magnetic field on the compass reading.
It varies with the boat's heading.

 b) Causes include: Ferromagnetic (iron and steel) objects such as engine, keel, hand-held flares, batteries, food or drink cans, some metal-frame glasses and so on.

  Electromagnetic influences such as from wire carrying electric current. Mobile phones.

  Magnetic influences such as from magnets found in loud speakers and some navigation instruments.

3.5

The bearing along the charted transit is 082°(T), add to this the local variation of 7°W = 089°(M).

The compass reading of 095°(C) is 6° greater than the magnetic; therefore the deviation is 6°(W).

3.6

50°21'.3N 004°28'.1W

The charted depth in this position is 46m so this makes sense.

Answer 3.6

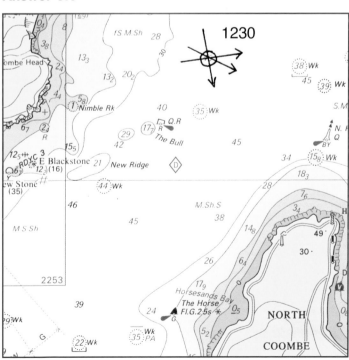

3.7

The old lighthouse on South Coombe Island should be clearly visible and a bearing could be taken.

The South Cardinal buoy would provide another position line. This is not good enough for a fix but a fix is not really necessary if everything seems to fit.

Monitoring the echo sounder will show a decrease in depth, followed by a large increase.

3.8

50°19'.15N 004°33'.05W

3.9

50°12'.0N 004°28'.25W

Confirmation could be obtained by introducing new data such as a visual bearing.

The South Cardinal buoy, which is almost on the beam and just over a mile away, will shortly come into transit with the old lighthouse on South Coombe Island.

An echo sounder reading will not help in this position.

3.10

a) The most likely reason for the poor quality of the fix is local magnetic anomalies in the area between Grand Lejon and Rohein, especially as Cap Frehel is at such long range.

b) The navigator can reduce the area of probability within the cocked hat by taking into account the depth reduced to soundings of 20.5 metres. This information places the boat outside the 20m contour line, effectively halving the area of probability.

Answer 3.7

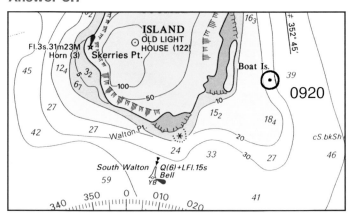

Answer 3.8

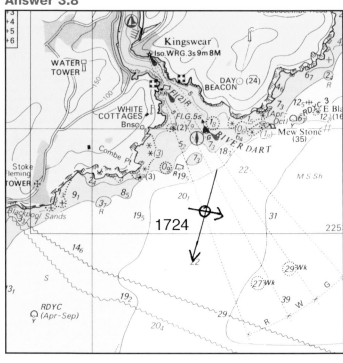

Answer 3.9

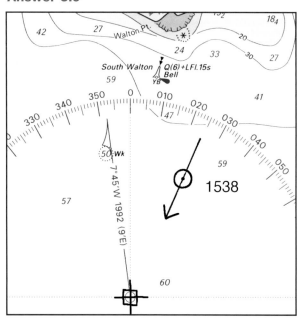

Answer 3.10

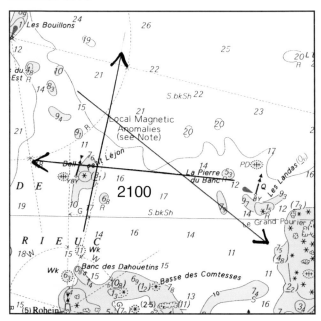

4.1

a) The Rules do not accord right of way to vessels.

Although vessels will alter course and speed as required by the Regulations, everyone at sea has an equal responsibility to avoid collision.

b) The Rules state that a good look-out should be kept at all times by all available means.

c) Early, in ample time.

d) Alter course to show the other vessel a different aspect, i.e. a different colour navigation light.

4.2

a) Vessel A, on port tack gives way, bearing away to pass astern of B or tacking, as appropriate.

b) Both A and B are required to make a manoeuvre. Each vessel turns to starboard they may also sound one short blast on the horn to indicate that they are turning.

c) As the vessels are on the same tack, the windward boat A should give way by bearing away to pass astern of B.

d) Vessel A on port tack gives way, bearing away to pass to leeward of B.

e) Crossing situation involving two powerboats, vessel B gives way by turning to pass behind A, or by slowing or stopping.

f) Yacht B is overtaking powerboat A, therefore the yacht must keep out of the way of the powerboat.

g) Powerboat B gives way, turning to pass behind yacht A.

h) Port tack yacht B gives way by tacking, because the tack of the other yacht is in doubt.

4.3

A risk of collision should be assumed if the compass bearing between approaching vessels does not appreciably change.

4.4

a) At anchor.

b) Vessel restricted in ability to manoeuvre.

c) Vessel constrained by draught.

d) Vessel engaged in fishing/trawling.

e) Motor sailing.

f) Vessel aground.

g) Vessel not under command.

4.5

a) When she is the windward boat to another sailing vessel on starboard tack.

When overtaking another vessel.

In a situation with:

a vessel restricted in her ability to manoeuvre.

a vessel not under command.

a vessel engaged in fishing/trawling.

Note: In addition, she must not impede ships in narrow channels or Traffic Separation Schemes or constrained by their draught.

b) i) Visibility.

ii) Traffic density.

iii) The manoeuvrability of the vessel.

iv) At night, the presence of background lights from the shore.

v) State of wind, sea and current.

vi) Navigational hazards.

vii) Draught in relation to the depth of water.

c) Heading

4.6

No. This combination of lights will be confusing to others because when looking at the port side of the yacht they would see a red light over a white one (the lights shown by fishing boats) and from the starboard side green over white (the lights shown by trawlers).

4.7

a) Sailing vessel, length unknown, starboard aspect.

b) Power-driven vessel, under 50m in length, seen from the port side, making way.

c) Power-driven vessel, probably over 50m in length, seen from dead ahead, making way.

d) Fishing vessel, probably under 50m, seen from the port side, making way.

e) Power-driven vessel, under 50m in length, restricted in ability to manoeuvre, seen from the starboard side, making way.

f) Sailing vessel, under 20m in length, seen from dead ahead.

g) Power-driven vessel, over 50m in length, length of tow greater that 200m, seen from the starboard side, making way.

h) Vessel over 50m in length, at anchor, seen from the starboard side.

i) Pilot vessel, length unknown, seen from the starboard side, making way.

j) Power-driven vessel, over 50m in length, constrained by her draught, seen from the port side, making way.

4.8

a) Power-driven vessel making way in restricted visibility; or, vessel approaching a blind bend.

b) Operating astern propulsion.

c) Power driven vessel in restricted visibility, underway but stopped and making no way through the water.

d) I am altering course to starboard.

e) In restricted visibility:

vessels not under command, vessels restricted in ability to manoeuvre, vessels constrained by draught, sailing vessels, vessels engaged in fishing or trawling, vessels engaged in towing or pushing.

f)   I am altering course to port.

g)   Vessel being towed in restricted visibility.

h)   I intend to overtake you on your starboard side.

i)   Vessel less than 100m at anchor in restricted visibility.

j)   I do not understand your intentions and do not believe you are taking sufficient action to avoid a collision.

4.9

a)   b)

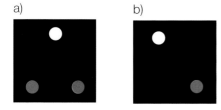

4.10

This is flag A, signifying that there are divers in the water. You should slow down and keep clear.

4.11

The safest course of action for the stand-on yacht is to turn away from the ship.

This manoeuvre has the advantages of reducing the relative rate of closing and of presenting the smallest possible target.

5.1

Any 4 from:

Smoking below, solvents and paints stored in the cabin, gas build-up in the bilges, faulty wiring, flames from cooking or petrol vapours.

5.2

a) The best way to avoid the build-up of leaked gas into the bilges is to fit a gas alarm, which should be regularly checked to ensure that it is functioning correctly. Make sure that the gas system has been fitted, and is maintained, correctly.

b) If a gas build-up is detected, open all the hatches and sail the boat downwind to allow fresh air to blow through the vessel.

Bilge pumps are designed to clear water not gas; many will not be effective in removing gas from the bilge.

5.3

a) Red parachute rocket. Fire slightly downwind to allow for the rocket climbing into the wind as it ascends.

b) White handheld flare. Hold horizontally and fire downwind for safety.

c) Red handheld flare. Hold horizontally and fire downwind for safety.

d) Orange handheld smoke or buoyant orange smoke.

5.4

a) Open the red cover and press for 5 seconds to send a distress alert. (Designate type of distress if there is time).

b) Mayday, Mayday, Mayday
This is yacht Azure, Azure, Azure
Mayday yacht Azure
MMSI (Include 9 digit number)
In position 50°11'.5N   004°38'.5W
Fire
Require immediate assistance
3 persons on board
Abandoning to liferaft
Over.

5.5

a) Any 3 from:

Send a Mayday. Check that the liferaft painter is tied on. Instruct the crew to wear lifejackets and warm clothes. Collect the grab bag or extra useful equipment if there is time.

b) When first launched, the raft is at its most unstable because the drogue has not been deployed, the bags beneath the raft are not yet full of water and there is no weight inside.

A heavy crew member inside will make the raft more stable and they will be able to assist others aboard from the vessel. All crew should try to stay dry if possible.

c) Once all the crew are aboard:

cut the painter, paddle away from the vessel, stream the drogue, close the door, take anti-seasickness tablets, keep as warm and dry as possible.

5.6

a) The boat should be about 30° to the wind on a port tack.

b) The hi-line is used to guide the winchman to the vessel. Do not touch the line until it has dipped in the water or touched the boat to discharge any static. It should not be tied to the vessel but should be used to pull the winchman aboard. Sailing gloves will protect the crew's hands and if the line is coiled into a bucket it will help prevent tangling of the rope. Be prepared to ease out on the line if necessary.

c) The foresail should be lowered and the mainsail lowered or reefed as directed by the crew of the helicopter. The engine should be started. All loose gear on the boat should be stowed and the crew briefed before the helicopter is overhead because then it will be too noisy. Remove aerials or danbuoys from the pushpit, especially on the port quarter where the winch man will approach the boat. The crew working on deck should wear lifejackets.

d) A rocket would be dangerous to the helicopter.

5.7

a) Search and Rescue Radar Transponder. This will pinpoint the position of the casualty vessel on the radar of any craft in the vicinity.

b) Emergency Position Indicating Radio Beacon. This will send a distress signal, via a satellite system to the Coastguard giving an approximate location. Some EPIRBs incorporate GPS for accurate positioning.

c) HM Coastguard.

5.8

a) Before it reaches the Angle of Vanishing Stability a vessel heeling over will right itself. Once beyond the AVS the vessel will roll over and become fully inverted.

b) The higher the AVS, the more likely the vessel is to resist becoming inverted and to right itself if it does invert.

5.9

Any 8 from:

Red handheld flare or red parachute rocket.
Orange smoke.
EPIRB.
Mayday.
Distress Alert from a VHF-DSC radio, or a SSB set.
A gun or other explosive signal.
A square flag with, above or below, a ball.
Continuous sound signal.
Raising and lowering outstretched arms.
SOS by light or sound ● ● ● ─ ─ ─ ● ● ●
Flames on the vessel.
Code flags N over C.

NOT internationally recognised are:

Sails or ensigns up side down.
Also note that a white flare is not a distress signal.

5.10

The information includes:

Gale and strong wind warnings, local weather forecast and parts of the shipping forecast.

Navigation warnings for the area.

Gunfacts and subfacts, messages about military firing and submarine activity in the area.

Buoyage & lights 6

6.1

Object such as buoys that are lit, are shown on the chart with a magenta tear drop.

6.2

This symbol shows the direction of buoyage.

6.3

a) South Cardinal buoy.

It would have a white light flashing 6 times followed by a long flash.

b) Red buoy.

Any light fitted would be red, flashing a different pattern from other red buoys in the vicinity.

6.4

a) Flashing green every 2^1/$_2$ seconds

b) A red occulting light (showing more light than dark), the light briefly goes out every 10 seconds.

c) White light flashing a morse letter. In this case U (• • ▬)

d) 2 fixed (non flashing) red lights, one above the other. This type of light is used on the end of piers and jetties.

6.5

Any 3 from:

North Cardinal, South Cardinal, East Cardinal, West Cardinal, Isolated Danger Mark and Safe Water Mark.

6.6

a) A white isophase light (showing equal periods of light and dark, in this case 1.5 seconds on and 1.5 seconds off) should be seen.

b) The colour of the light will change to green. The characteristic will remain the same.

c) The buoy should be left on the starboard side of the boat.

6.7

a) A white light flashing twice usually every 10 seconds. Fl.(2) 10s.

b) A white light flashing 3 times every 5 or 10 seconds.

c) A yellow flashing light.

d) A white light flashing continuously.

6.8

a) A Safe Water Mark, used to show the beginning of a buoyed channel.

b) A white light often a long flash every 10 seconds (L.Fl.10s.)
   It could also be isophase, occulting or morse code A (• ▬).

6.9

a) West Cardinal, turn to starboard.

b) Preferred channel to starboard.

6.10

a) White; light flashing group two every ten seconds. Red; fixed light (on all the time).

b) No; only the white light is visible (360°) from Plymouth Sound. The red light has a fairly narrow sector as shown on the chart.

c) White light; 41 metres. Red light; 28 metres. Lights measured above Mean High Water Springs.

d) The nominal range of the light does not take into account the curvature of the Earth. With a low height of eye (as from a small craft) it's likely that the light will be below the horizon at the charted range.

7.1

b) Wind blowing against the direction of the tidal stream.

7.2

The term tidal gate refers to a time period for a given sea area, which can be expected to have particularly strong tidal streams. As a consequence, navigators of relatively slow boats plan to reach such areas when the tidal stream is favourable in order to maintain an efficient speed over the ground (SOG).

A good example of a tidal gate is the Race of Alderney where the tidal drift (rate) can be in excess of 7.0 knots at spring tides.

7.3

a) 046°(T) 2.5 knots.

b) 192°(T) 0.8 knots.

c) 061°(T) 1.05 knots.

7.4

a) Friday 9th August   HW Plymouth   1500 BST neap range   HW + 2 050°(T) 0.7 knot

b) Friday 5th July   HW Plymouth   0954 BST spring range HW + 6 222°(T) 1.0 knot

c) Thursday 13th June HW Plymouth   0429 BST mid range   HW   039°(T) 0.8 knot

7.5

a) 058°(T) 2.0 knots

b) Saturday 25th May   HW Plymouth   1128 BST neap range   HW – 4   284°(T) 1.3 knots

c) Monday 10th June HW Plymouth   0120 BST mid range

   Tidal stream turns between 5 and 6 hours after HW   0650

d) Tuesday 23rd July HW Plymouth   1108 BST mid range

   Tidal stream turns between 2 and 1 hours before HW   0938

7.6

Monday 24th June HW Plymouth 1146 BST neaps

Tidal stream is at its minimum rate during the HW hour 1115 to 1215

7.7

Saturday 31st August   HW Plymouth   0827 BST   Range springs +

The range is 5.5m or 5.4m, well above the mean spring range of 4.7m so the tidal streams will be stronger than the average information given in the atlas or on the chart. With the wind in the SW there will be dangerously rough conditions in the Race if the boat goes through at the wrong time.

The boat should be approaching the Race 1$^1/_2$ hours before HW, at 0657 BST.

7.8

a) Wednesday 31st January   HW Plymouth   1455 UT   Range 2.2m (neaps)

HW – 5   0925 – 1025   216°(T)   2.5 knots

HW – 4   1025 – 1125   214°(T)   2.0 knots

b) Monday 1st July   HW Plymouth   0631 BST   Range 4.7m (springs)

HW + 1   0701 – 0801   018°(T)   2.4 knots for $^1/_2$ hour 1.2M

HW + 2   0801 – 0901   349°(T)   3.0 knots for $^1/_2$ hour 1.5M

c) Saturday 16th March   HW Plymouth   0245 UT   Range 3.4m (mid)

HW + 2   0415 – 0515   085°(T)   3.6sp   1.8np   Int 2.7 knots

HW + 3   0515 – 0615   086°(T)   3.2sp   1.6np   Int 2.4 knots for $^1/_2$ hour 1.2M

Tidal heights 8

8.1

a) LW.

b) Chart datum.

c) Height of tide.

d) Green.

e) MHWS.

8.2

a) Height of tide 2.5m + charted depth 5.2m = 7.7m.

b) Height of tide 2.5m – drying height 0.5m = 2.0m.

8.3

a) Charted depth 7.2m + MLWS 0.7m = 7.9m.

b) MLWN 2.0m – drying height 0.9m = 1.1m.

8.4

a) 0457   5.1m

b) 2125   11.9m

c) 0823   12.9m

   (It is not necessary to add an hour because zone time is the same as BST)

8.5

a) 4.7m   spring range.

b) 2.3m   neap range.

c) 3.4m   mid range.

8.6

a) HW 11.5m   LW1.0m   spring range   Ht of tide 8.5m

b) HW 4.4m   LW 2.0m neap range   Ht of tide 3.0m

8.7

Tuesday 4th June   HW Plymouth 0826 BST 5.4m   LW 0.5m   spring range

Height of tide at 0630 = 4.7m

8.8

Wednesday 8th May   HW Plymouth   1009   5.0m   LW 1.2m   Range 3.8m

a) Height of tide at 1230 BST: 4.0m

b) Tide will fall: 4.0m – 1.2m = 2.8m

c) Minimum depth to anchor in at 1230 BST: fall + draught + clearance = 5.4m

8.9

Sunday 28th July HW St Helier 1750 BST 9.9m LW 2.0m mid range

Height of tide at 2040 BST: 6.7m

Tide will fall: 6.7m − 2.0m = 4.7m

Depth of water − fall − draught = clearance of 0.3m

No. This is not a safe clearance.

8.10

a) April

	Time		Height	
	HW	LW	HW	LW
Standard port – Plymouth	0600	1300	5.5	0.8
Secondary port – Brixham	+ 0045	+ 0010	- 0.6	- 0.1
BST adjustment	+ 0100	+ 0100		
	0745	1410	4.9m	0.7m

b) June

	Time		Height	
	HW	LW	HW	LW
Standard port – Saint Helier	1200	1730	9.5	2.7
Secondary port – Braye (Alderney)	+ 0045	+ 0045	- 4.1	-1.0
BST adjustment	+ 0100	+ 0100		
	1345	1915	5.4m	1.7m

c) August

	Time		Height	
	HW	LW	HW	LW
Standard port – Saint Malo	2206	0518	10.6	2.6
Secondary port – Carteret	+ 0029	+ 0027	- 1.3	- 0.4
BST adjustment (Not required zone time = BST)				
	2235	0545	9.3m	2.2m

8.11

a) Sunday 21st July

	Time		Height	
	HW	LW	HW	LW
Standard port – Plymouth	0857	0240	4.8	1.3
Secondary port – Torquay	+ 0037	+ 0007	- 0.7	- 0.1
BST adjustment	+ 0100	+ 0100		
	1034	0347	4.1m	1.2m

b) Tuesday 9th January

	Time		Height	
	HW	LW	HW	LW
Standard port – Plymouth	2002	1351	5.0	1.2
Secondary port – Start Point	+ 0023	- 0003	- 0.3	- 0.1
BST adjustment				
	2025	1348	4.7m	1.1m

c) Monday 13th May

	Time		Height	
	HW	LW	HW	LW
Standard port – Saint Helier	1530	2205	9.2	2.5
Secondary port – Braye	+ 0049	+ 0056	- 3.9	- 0.9
BST adjustment	+ 0100	+ 0100		
	1719	0001	5.3m	1.6m

8.12

Monday 15th April   Range ³/₄ springs

	Time HW	Height HW	LW
Standard port – Plymouth	1603	5.1	0.9
Secondary port – Brixham	+ 0037	- 0.6	- 0.1
BST adjustment	+ 0100		
	1740	4.5m	0.8m

Height of tide from the graph at 2000	3.5
Height of tide at LW	- 0.8
Fall of tide	2.7
Draft	1.6
Clearance	2.0
Depth of water to anchor in at 2000 BST	6.3m

8.13

Sunday 30th June   Range ³/₄ springs

	Time HW	HW	Height HW	LW	HW
Standard port – Saint Malo	0559	1824	11.4	1.9	12.0
Secondary port – Carteret	+ 0028	+ 0027	- 1.5	- 0.3	- 1.6
BST adjustment					
	0627	1851	9.9m	1.6m	10.4m

a)
Height of tide from the graph at 0925	6.8
Depth of water at 0925	- 2.8
Drying height	4.0
Draft	+ 1.5
Vessel will ground when tide falls to	5.5m

From the graph: 1010 BST

b) Yes. The area dries to a height of 4.0m, LW today is 1.6m therefore the boat will dry by 2.4m.

c) The vessel will re-float when the height of tide rises to 5.5m again. From the graph, 1600 BST.

Chartwork position 9

Answers 9.1

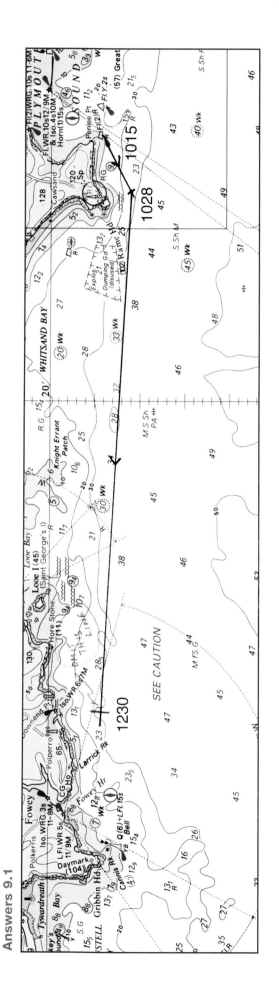

Answer 9.2

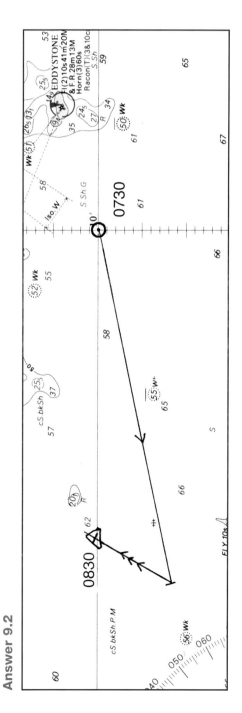

9.1

50°18'.8N   005°30'.6W

9.2

a)   50°10'.1N   005°30'.4W

b)   Speed over ground 6.6 knots

c)   Course over ground 271°(T)

9.3

a) HW Plymouth 1804 BST. Spring range.

b) HW – 5   280°(T) 2.3 knots.

c) 50°15′.3N   005°04′.2W.

d) Speed through the water on the log 5.2 knots.

e) Speed over ground 7.3 knots. Course over ground 296°(T).

9.4

a) 50°14′.0N   005°14′.0W.

b) The boat will pass about 0.7 of a mile north of the shallowest area.

c) The boat will pass the buoy in about 40 minutes, at 1515 BST.

9.5

a) HW Plymouth 1500 BST.   Neap range.

b) HW +1 hour   098°(T)   1.6 knots.

c) EP 49°52′.0N 004°53′.6W   The yacht will be outside the area by 0.4 miles.

d) The buoy will be on the port side of the boat.

9.6

Red.

Answer 9.3

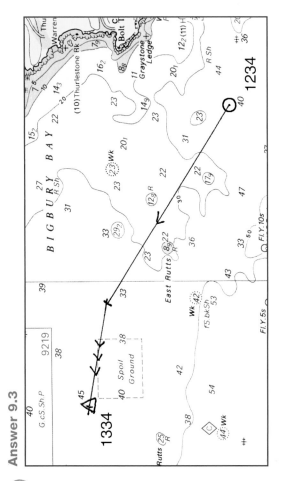

Answers 9.4

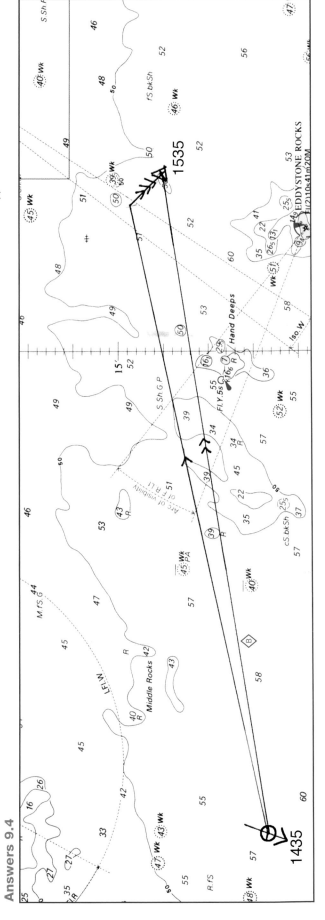

Answer 9.5

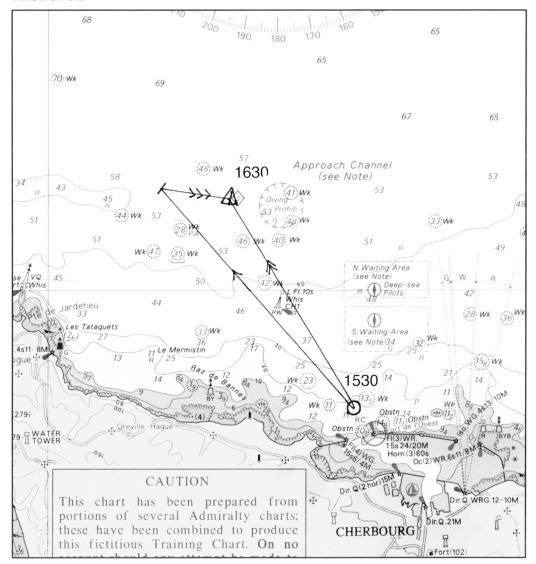

Answer 9.6

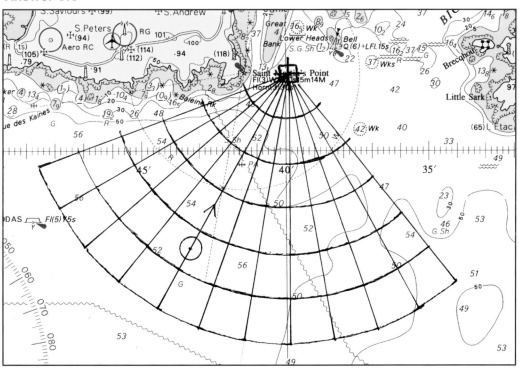

9.7

Course	290°(M)
Variation	- 7°W
	283°(T)

Sunday 28th April   HW Plymouth   1456 BST
Range 2.2m neaps

HW 1426 – 1526   032°(T)   2.6 knots

EP at 1525: 49°41'.8N   005°27'.1W

Comment; the course over ground (COG) of 304°(T)
passes over the 8.8 metre charted depth at the
southern end of the Banc de Schôle.

9.8

Fix: 49°47'.3N   005°24'.7W

Course	140°(C)
Deviation	+ 6°E
	146°(M)
Variation	- 7°W
	139°(T)

Monday 13th May   HW Plymouth 1540 BST
Range 3.4m

The area in question is midway between two sets
of tidal stream data. For the period 1210 -1310
(HW-3), the stream through the Alderney Race is
205° 2.3 knots (neaps) and 5.7 knots (springs).
At the same time, the stream between Alderney and
Guernsey is 205° 1.0 knots (neaps) and 2.3 knots
(springs).

Without local knowledge, it is best to interpolate
between these figures, so:
at neaps, it is between 2.3 knots and 1.0 knots,
i.e. 1.7 knots
at springs, it is between 2.3 knots and 5.7 knots,
i.e. 4.0 knots
midway between neaps and springs, it is 2.8 knots,
i.e. 1.4 miles in 1/2 hour.

EP at 1240 BST 49°41'.5N   5°19'.7W
SOG 13.4 knots COG 150°(T)

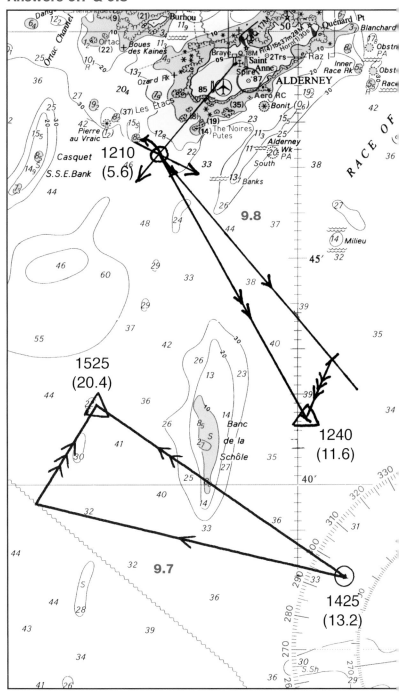

9.9

Course   345°(C)
Deviation   - 5°W
                            340°(M)
Variation   - 7°W
                            333°(T)

Monday 1st July HW Plymouth   0631 BST   Range 4.7m springs

HW + 1 0701 – 0801 046°(T)   4.0 knots

    a)   49°59'.5N   005°42'.8W

    b)   SOG 13.7 knots   COG 349°(T)

    c) $\dfrac{\text{Distance 9.7 M}}{\text{SOG}\quad 13.7 \text{ kn}} \times 60 = 42 \text{ minutes}$

Answer 9.9

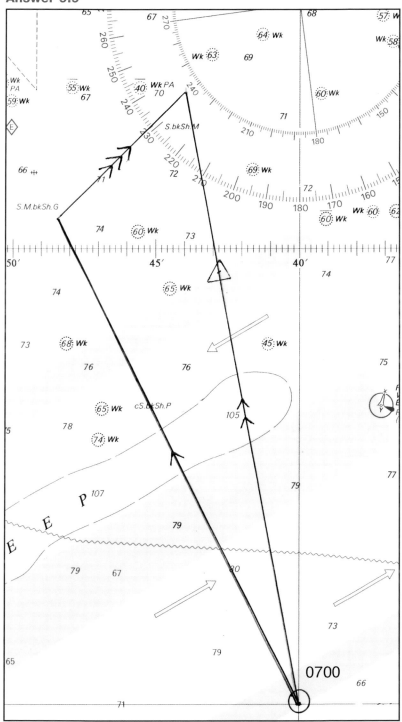

9.10

Port tack:	Course	045°(C)	Starboard tack:	Course	315°(C)
	Deviation	nil		Deviation	- 6°W
		045°(M)			309°(M)
	Variation	- 7°W		Variation	- 7°W
		038°(T)			302°(T)
	Leeway	+ 5°		Leeway	- 5°
		043°(T)			297°(T)

Tuesday 16th April   HW Plymouth   1751 BST   Range 4.7m springs

HW – 1 1621 – 1721 063°(T) 2.2 knots for $^1/_2$ = 1.1M for each tack

COG on port tack: 048°(T)

COG on starboard tack: 314°(T)

The yacht will clear the overfalls.

Answer 9.10

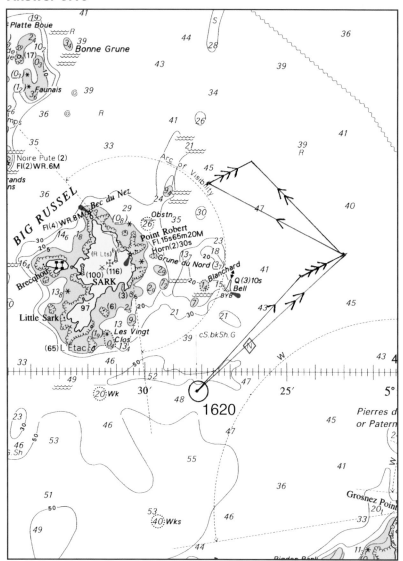

9.11

Fix: 49°47'.3N   005°44'.5W

9.12

a) See chart below.

b) Course   065°(C)
Deviation   + 2°E
                         067°(M)
Variation   - 7°W
                         060°(T)

Tuesday 30th April HW Plymouth   1645 BST   Range 3.4m

HW – 5 1115 – 1215 225°(T)   4.7sp   2.1np   Int 3.4 knots

ii) 0.5M to starboard, steer left.

c) 035°(T) 2.1 miles.

d) Due to the effect of the tidal stream the COG passes close to the charted eddies at Eight Fathom Ledge where the skipper should expect confused seas. It also passes less than a mile to the north of the Casquets rocks, which could be considered a doubtful decision.

It would have been advisable for the skipper to have monitored the XTE and adjust the course in order to stay closer to the original rhumb line. This would have kept the vessel about a mile off the TSS to the north, while at the same time keeping her outside the 50 metre contour around the Casquets.

Answers 9.11 & 9.12

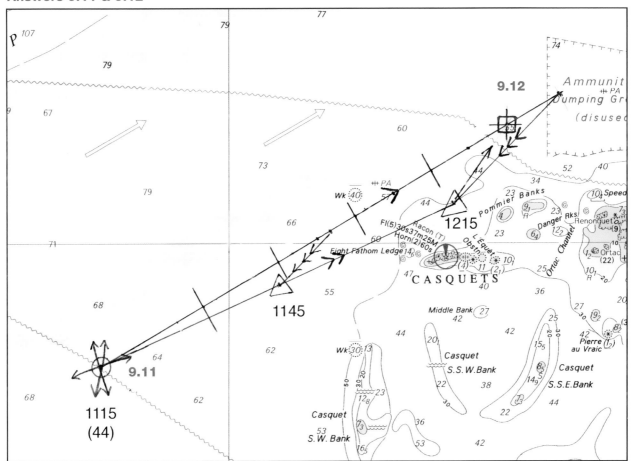

10.1

a) 8.1 miles.

b) Course to steer 026°(T)   033°(M)

c) Just less than an hour.

d) The buoy will be seen off the starboard bow because of the heading of the boat.

Answer 10.1

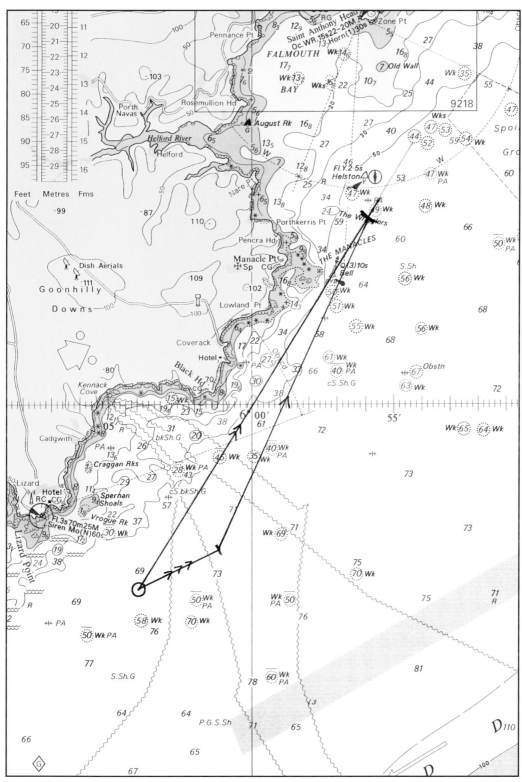

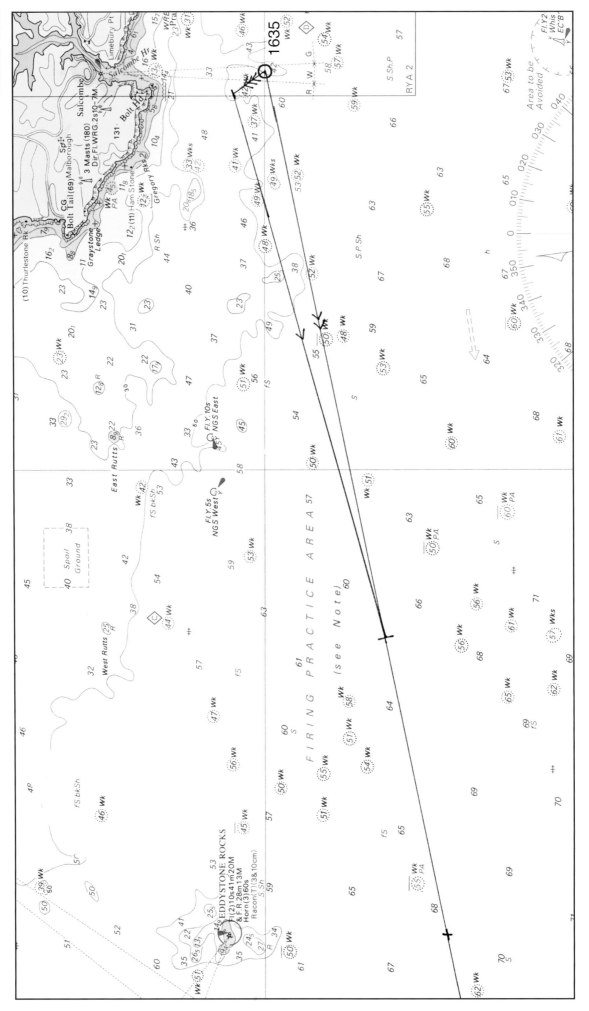

10.2

The distance to travel is approximately 19.5 miles so it will take about ³/₄ hour at 25 knots.

A plot for ¹/₂ hour, ³/₄ hour or 1 hour should give the same answer.

¹/₂ hour diagram shown overleaf. Course to steer   253°(T)   260°(M)

10.3

a) Sunday 4th August   HW Plymouth   1017 BST   spring range

b) HW – 4 hours   278°(T)   2.3 knots

c) Course to steer: 022°(T)   029°(M)

d) The buoy will be seen well over on the port bow because of the strong tidal stream.

No. The helmsman should not alter course. Checks should be made with the hand-bearing compass when the buoy is sighted before any decisions are made.

If the buoy's position had been put into the GPS as a waypoint then a check could have been made using the cross track error information.

Answer 10.3

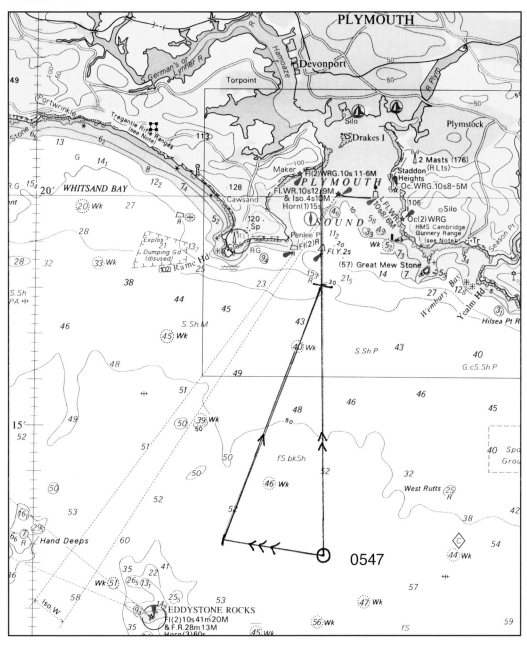

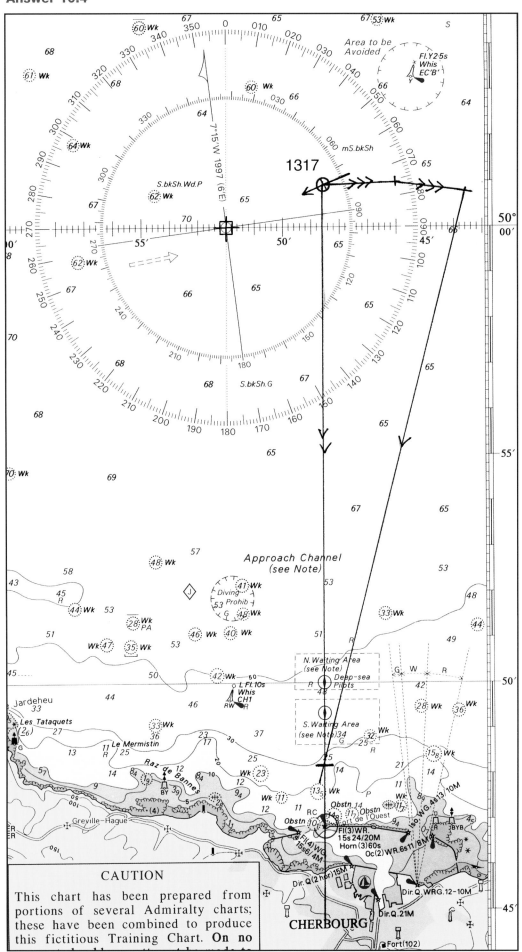

10.4

Monday 27th May   HW Plymouth   1347 BST   neap range

a) Tidal stream charts: HW   089°(T)   1.6 knots

   HW +1   098°(T)   1.6 knots

b) Course to steer 195°(T)   202°(M)

c) To allow for the leeway head up into the wind to 207°(M)

10.5

See plot on page 84.

Position at 1920 BST: 49°55'.75N 004°58'.6W

Friday 17th May   HW Plymouth   1848 BST   Range 4.6m

⟨J⟩   HW + 1   1918 – 2018 BST   098°(T)   3.4sp for ¹/₂ hour   1.7M

a) Course to steer   155°(T)
   Variation   + 7°W
                          162°M
   Deviation   - 5°E
                          157°(C)   SOG 17.0 knots   COG 145°(T)

b) Yes. As the predicted tidal streams are constant during this ¹/₂ hour vector the boat should proceed (theoretically) down the ground track. This means the bearing to waypoint displayed by the GPS will remain constant.

10.6

See plot on page 84

Fix at 2100 BST: 49°51'.5N 005°19'.8W

Wednesday 22nd May   HW Plymouth 2129 BST   Range 3.5 mid range

Tidal stream charts: HW 2059 – 2159 BST   049°(T)   2.1np   5.0sp Int 3.6kn

Course to steer   093°(T)
Variation   + 7°W
                   100°(M)
Deviation   - 4°E
                   096°(C)

$$\frac{\text{Distance to go 12.9M}}{\text{SOG \qquad 14.9kn}} \times 60 = 52 \text{ min} + 2100 = \text{ETA 2152 BST}$$

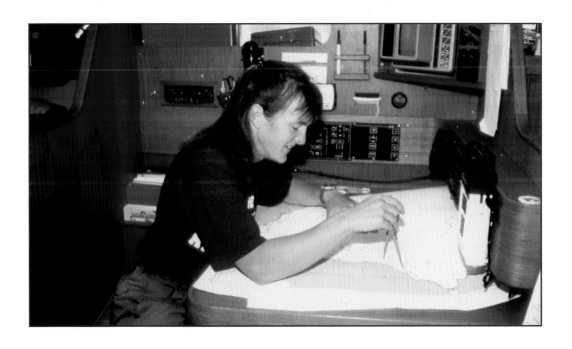

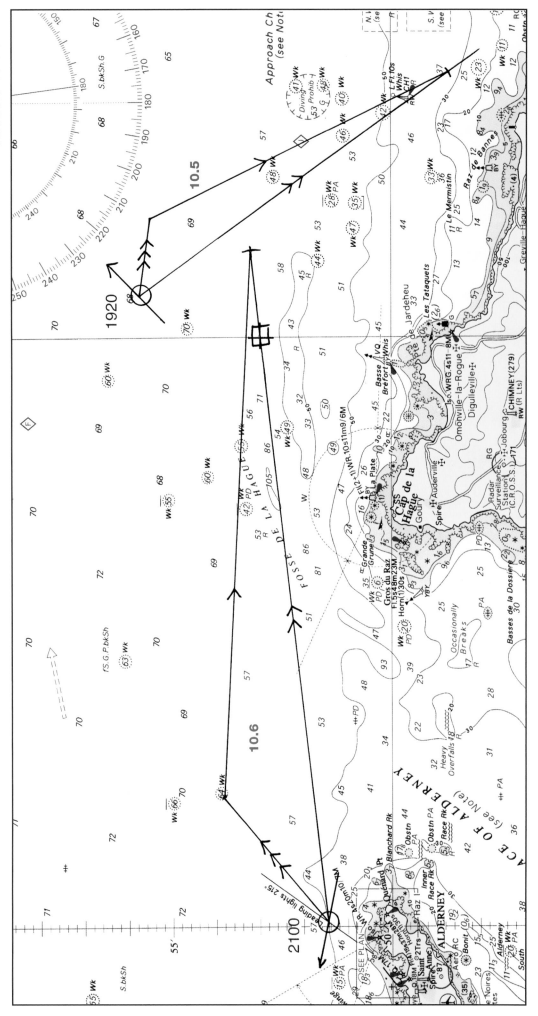

10.7

Position at 1900 BST 49°43'.6N 005°13.5W

Saturday 1st June   HW Plymouth   1827 BST   Range 4.7 springs

Tidal stream charts: HW + 1 1857 – 1957 BST 002°(T) 2.3sp x ¹/₂ hour 1.15M

a) Course to steer   123°(T)
Variation   + 7°W
                       130°(M)
Deviation   − 6°E
                       124°(C)   SOG 17.4kn   COG 115°(T)

b) i)   The XTE would start to increase, indicating that the boat was off track.

ii) The bearing to waypoint would change, decreasing in this example if the drift of the tide weakened but the set remained the same.

iii) The SOG would increase if the tidal drift weakened but the set remained the same.

Answer 10.7

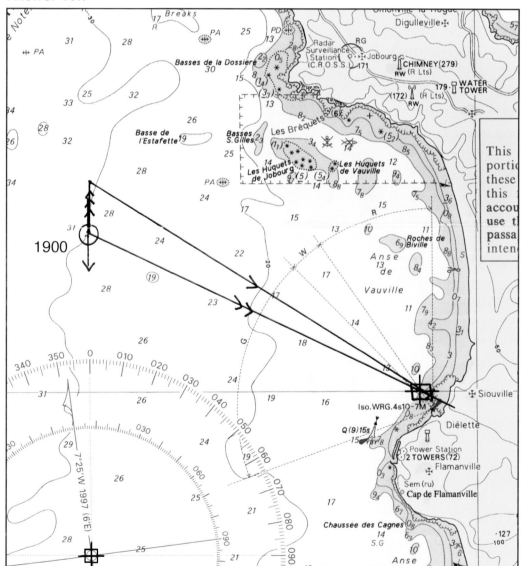

10.8

Wednesday 24th January   HW Plymouth 2054 UT   Range 4.7m springs

⟨E⟩ HW + 1   2124 – 2224 UT   055°(T)   1.4 sp

HW + 2   2224 – 2324 UT   061°(T)   1.4 sp

a) Course to steer   285°(T)
   Variation   + 7°W
                          292°(M)
   Leeway   + 10°
                          302°(M)
   ETA 2341 UT
   Deviation   + 5°W
                          307°(C)

$$\frac{\text{Distance to go}\quad 11.6M}{\text{SOG}\qquad\qquad 5.1kn} \times 60 = 2hr\ 16mins + 2125$$

b) If the leeway proved to be greater than estimated, the XTE would indicate that the boat had drifted to port of the track. As this happened the bearing to waypoint would begin to increase.

Answer 10.8

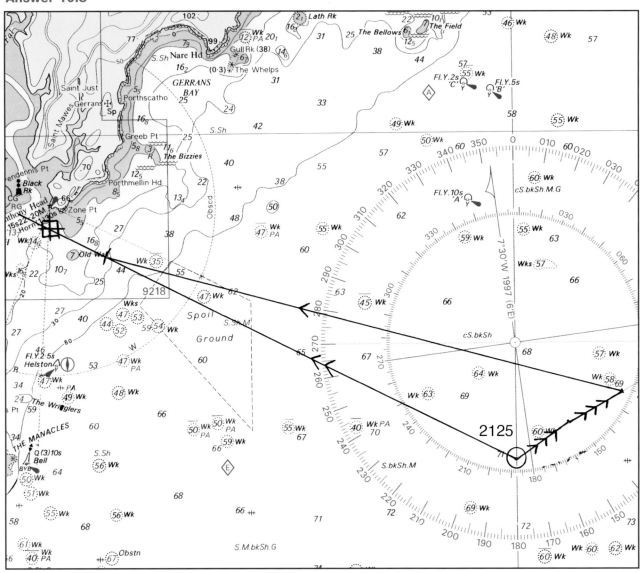

Electronic navigation aids 11

11.1

b) Speed through the water.

11.2

1) A towed log that is streamed behind the vessel. This kind of log is often to be found onboard ocean cruising yachts, where it finds favour due to its simplicity. It is quite susceptible to becoming fouled by sea weed and has been known to be eaten by large ocean fish!

2) Sonic log. This kind of log has no moving parts which means that the problem of it becoming fouled doesn't occur.

11.3

A log that under reads. Landfall would be made sooner than expected which could be dangerous, especially with off lying shoals and rocks.

11.4

c) Depth sounders can normally be calibrated to show either.

11.5

The wash from passing ships can create a mass of air bubbles in the water. As they are good reflectors of sound the instrument displays a mass of shallow readings, or no depth at all, until the water is has become less turbulent.

11.6

c) Navigators can expect the GPS system to be accurate to within 15 metres 95% of the time.

11.7

a) The bearing and range from the vessel to the waypoint and the latitude and longitude displayed will be at the same position.

Navigators often find it easier to plot position with reference to bearing and range. Placing a waypoint at the centre of a compass rose gives a practical advantage too, as the true bearing to the waypoint can be seen at a glance, especially useful when underway.

b) The TTG (time to go) shown on the display is 47 minutes + 1113 = ETA of 1200.

c) ii) On an open water passage such as crossing the channel it's often best to allow the boat to be swept one way by the tidal stream, then back again. This will mean that during the passage the XTE may become quite large. This isn't a problem so long as the navigator has checked that the vessel isn't going to be swept into danger.

This is not the case when piloting through a narrow water way such as the Little Russel, where XTE would need to be kept to a minimum in order to avoid the rocks.

d) If the XTE started to increase this would be indicated by the vessel icon (small black dot) moving to one side or the other of the broken line shown in the middle of the rolling road.

e) i) 100°(T) 2.5 knots. The displayed speed over ground (SOG) is greater than the speed through the water indicating that the tide is adding to the vessel's speed. The opposite would have been the case had the set and drift been 310°(T) 3.5 knots.

f) The HdoP (Horizontal Dilution of Precision) display indicates when the satellites are too close together for a highly accurate fix. The number 1.5 indicates a good fix in this example. Double figures mean poorer accuracy.

g) The SOG and VMG in this example are the same because the boat is progressing down the ground track, directly toward the waypoint. If this were a yacht tacking toward the waypoint, (for example) the VMG and SOG would be different.

11.8

Back up: visual bearings, transits, charted objects, depth, course and distance run, radar range and bearings. Recording position regularly in boat's log and chart.

11.9

i) Raster: a) and c)   ii) Vector: b), d), e) and f)

11.10

When a chart is over magnified it can give the impression that the resolution of position improves as the scale becomes larger. However, with the increasing reliability and accuracy of GPS, there is every likelihood that the actual latitude and longitude of the vessel is far more accurate than the chart on which it is being displayed.

11.11

a) As the radar's range is unaffected by changes in the vessel's heading, it is likely to provide a more reliable position line. This is especially true in heavy seas, when the boat may be swinging from one side of a given heading to the other.

b) Depending on the radar's beam width, typically around 5° or 6° for small craft radar, it may not be able to pick out a narrow entrance. This is because the width of the beam effectively paints across a small gap on the radar screen, hiding it from view.

c) With the range decreasing and the bearing steady (or nearly steady) you should be alerted to the risk of collision with the target.

12.1

a) Vessel may proceed. Two way traffic.

iii)

b) A vessel may proceed when she has received specific orders to do so, except that vessels which navigate outside the main channel need not comply with the main message.

ii)

c) Serious emergency all vessels to stop or divert according to instructions.

i)

FLASHING

12.2

a) Steer to port.
b) Green.

12.3

a) A back bearing of 072°(M) on the Skerries Point lighthouse will keep the vessel clear of the charted overfalls. If the bearing increases the boat will have strayed too far north, if the bearing decreases then she will be further south than she needs to be, although at least in safe water.

b) A bearing of more than 005°(M) shows that the boat has passed to the west of the overfalls.

12.4

a) All the visitors buoys are white and marked FHC VISITORS.

b) No. Do not attempt the rocky passage except with local knowledge and at HW.

c) When the tide reaches 3.0 metres the gates stay open for free-flow.

d) To the west of the harbour are anchorages in Fishcombe Cove and Elbery Cove, beware of water skiers.

e) The lights may be difficult to discern against the town's lights.

f) A boat with a 1.5 metre draft can stay afloat for 6 hours at neap tide.

g) A water tower (43m) is conspicuous 6 cables NNW of the entrance to Portbail (1 cable = $^1/_{10}$ of a nautical mile).

h) Depth over the sill is shown on a lit digital display atop the south breakwater, it can be hard to read in bright sunlight.

12.5

In thick fog, the anglers will want to stay out of the main channel in order to reduce the risk of collision. At 1520 the tidal stream is favourable for returning to the River Dart, the height of tide is approximately 4.4m.

By using their depth sounder to follow the 20m contour line, they will be able to safely pilot the boat back to the river. A keen look-out will have to be maintained to avoid the unlit port-hand buoy off the NE tip of the Skerries Bank, but they may be able to hear its bell which will help confirm their position.

12.6

a) 1135 BST is three hours after HW Salcombe. With a height of tide of more than 3.0m it might at first glance, look feasible to cross the Bar and enter Salcombe. However it's mid ebb on a big spring tide (range 5.3m), this means that there will be a wind against tide situation in the area, this coupled with the heavy swell is likely to produce very rough and confused seas over the bar.

b) Advice about conditions at the bar is available by calling Salcombe's Harbour Master on VHF Channel 14, this should be done before approaching.

12.7

The skipper can be confident that the buoy has drifted out of position, because the white sector of Saint Anthony Head light is in view. When the buoy is in the correct position it lays within the red sector of the light.

12.8

a) At HW + 2 (1200 BST) the tidal stream will be setting toward the east.

b) A bearing of 002°(T) (009°(M)) on S.Werburgh's church tower clears the rocks.

c) Leading beacons ashore (white triangles with black stripes) in line at 089°(T) (096°(M)) show the navigator when to turn towards the river, keeping the boat clear of Mouthstone Ledge, but not the sand bar.

d) A port hand marker buoy, Fl.R5s (April – October) marks the end of the sand bar which must be left to port on entry.

e) Once passed the sand bar, and abeam the beacon (green triangle on a white square) on the south shore, turn NE towards a beacon on the north shore (white square with red stripe).

f) No. At 1600 it will be practically low water springs. From the sand bar to Misery Point the river carries only 1.2m of water at this state of tide.

g) No. The wind is easterly and the pilotage notes say that it is impossible to beat in against an ebb tide.

13.1

b). The anticlockwise wind circulation indicates low pressure in the Northern Hemisphere.

13.2

c). By delaying departure until the low has passed it's likely that they will need to change their plans. Better to have a safe, enjoyable weekend around the local ports than to needlessly venture out into bad weather.

13.3

(a) Beaufort Force 5, 17 – 21 knots.

(b) Beaufort Force 7 (near gale), 28 – 33 knots.

13.4

a) Imminent: timing, within 6 hrs from time of issue.

b) Veering: wind changing in a clockwise direction.

c) Good: visibility, greater than 5 miles.

d) Severe gale: high waves, spray affects visibility, wind speed 41 – 47 knots.

e) Fair: no significant precipitation.

f) Later: timing, after 12 hrs from time of issue.

g) Fog: visibility, less than 1,000 metres.

13.5

With the yacht running before a westerly breeze, Buys Ballot's Law puts the low to the north, in the Northern Hemisphere.

13.6

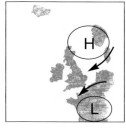

a) ENE Strong.

b) SW Strong.

c) WSW Light.

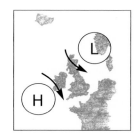

d) NW Strong.

e) ENE Light.

f) NNW Moderate.

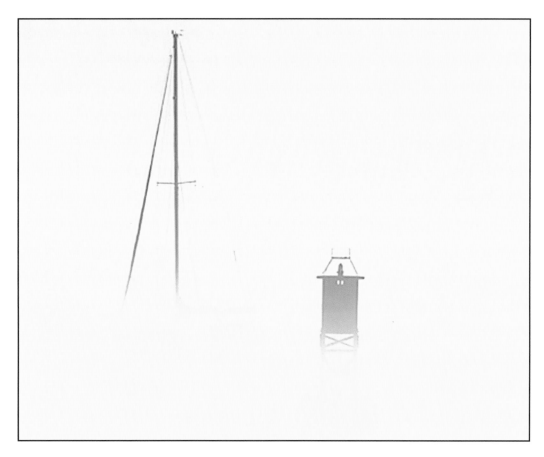

13.7

a) Radiation or land fog: often occurs during settled weather in autumn and winter.

 The land cools down quickly which in turn cools the air above it. When the air is cooled below its capacity to hold moisture as vapour, the moisture condenses and forms fog.

b) Advection or sea fog: occurs when warm moist air blows over a colder sea, the cold sea cools the air below its capacity to hold the moisture as a vapour, enabling the moisture to condense and form fog.

 Most common in late winter and spring, when northern seas are at their coldest.

13.8

a) Fair Isle

b) The English Channel is under the warm sector of the system; low cloud, predominately fracto/alto stratus, patchy drizzle or light rain and a steady SW wind, Force 5.

c) Warm front.

d) With the cold front running down the Irish sea, Ireland has the bright and breezy conditions with blustery showers.

e) The weather map shows tightly spaced isobars in the vicinity of Viking, indicating strong winds in that area. The isobars over Biscay are further apart showing there are lighter winds there.

13.9

As the summer morning progresses, the sun will heat the land. This in turn will warm up the air above it, which will start to rise, allowing cooler, denser air from over the sea to blow on shore.

Expect this on shore coastal breeze to start from mid-morning, continuing into the afternoon.

Once night falls the localised heating of the land will stop, along with the sea breeze. As the land cools the air above it will also cool, flowing downhill and out to sea, resulting in a light land breeze for a time.

Passage planning 14

14.1

Friday 21st June   HW Plymouth   2150 BST   Range 3.4m

◇D⟩ HW – 5   1620 – 1720   226°(T)   2.3sp   1.1np   Int 1.7kn

The tidal stream is setting southwest, and the skipper will want to lee bow the tide, making port tack advantageous.

14.2

Monday.
The forecast of northeasterly winds will make Braye Harbour very uncomfortable, sail past Alderney and make for Saint Helier.

Tuesday.
The easterly breeze presents an opportunity for a pleasant reach over to Saint Malo.

Wednesday.
Gale force southerly winds make staying at Saint Malo the best option.

Thursday.
Sail North on the southwesterly breeze to Braye Harbour on Alderney.

Friday.
Sailing back to Plymouth is likely to be the best plan for Friday.

Returning via Cherbourg isn't a good plan, as this would place the vessel downwind for the passage back.

14.3

HW Plymouth is at approximately 1830 BST. The vessels get underway at 1900 when the tidal stream charts show the set and drift to be foul for a passage to Jersey.

With a maximum speed of 5.0 knots while towing, they will need to make for Saint Peter Port.

14.4

i) Overall distance, approximately 25M.

ii) HW Plymouth on the 13th May: 0300 BST   Range 3.1m.

At 2030 BST (departure time) the tidal stream charts show favourable set and drift for the next four hours. The tidal lift during the passage will be roughly 3 or 4 miles, with a boat speed of 5.0kn the passage will take approximately 4 hours.

iii) ETA at Salcombe: 0030 BST

iv) Plymouth Monday 13th May

	Time	Height	
	HW	HW	LW
	0200 UT	4.8m	1.7m
Correction Salcombe	+ 02	- 0.3m	- 0.1m
	0202	4.5m	1.6m
	+ 0100		
Salcombe BST	0302		

Height of tide from the graph at 0030 BST	3.8m
Charted depth at The Bar	1.0m +
Depth of water at The Bar at 0030 BST	4.8m
Vessels draft	1.7m −
Clearance	3.1m

v) Care will be required to avoid ships in the channel, also towards the latter part of the passage the overfalls off Start Point will need to be taken into account.

vi) leg 1.   145°(T)   3.75M

leg 2.   198°(T)   3.5M

leg 3.   198°(T)   3.15M

leg 4.   205°(T)   3.95M

leg 5.   222°(T)   2.85M

leg 6.   263°(T)   6.1M

leg 7.   358°(T)   1.55M

14.5

Both skippers are correct.

HW Plymouth is at 1545 BST, the tidal stream charts show that at 1115 the set is predominantly towards the west. The skipper of the planing hull powerboat needs to leave soon in order to have wind and tide together for the passage. This will give the smoothest sea conditions, enabling cruising speed to be maintained.

The yacht skipper will have to wait until the tide turns at 1415 BST.

Due to the comparatively low boat speed of the yacht, it's important to have tidal assistance on this passage.

14.6

i) Weather: before departure, check the weather forecast and get regular updates while at sea.

ii) Tides: check the tidal height and stream predictions for the passage and ensure the plan fits in with them.

iii) Vessel: consider whether the boat is up to the proposed trip, and make sure that there is sufficient safely equipment and stores onboard.

iv) Crew: take into account the experience and ability of the crew, Tired or seasick crew members could overburden the skipper.

v) Navigational dangers: consult up-to-date charts, pilot books and publications to ensure that you are familiar with any navigational dangers that might be met while on route.

vi) Contingency plans: prepare a plan which will enable you to take advantage of any bolt holes or ports of refuge along the way.

vii) Contacts ashore: tell someone ashore of your plans, and make sure they know what to do if they become concerned for your welfare. The Coastguard (CG66) Safety Identification Scheme is also useful as it can help the Coastguard respond quickly should you be in trouble.

15.1

a) HW Plymouth 0738 BST 5.4m 0.6m spring range

b) Access HW Salcombe +/- 4$^{1}/_{2}$ hours. 0317 – 1217 BST

c) The distance is approximately 25 miles, so passage time is about 4 hours, less with tidal assistance.

d) The tidal streams become favourable between 1 hour before HW and HW until between 3 and 4 hours after HW. 0708 to 1108 BST.

e) No. There is access to Torquay at any state of the tide, day or night.

f) Yes. The wind will be just behind the beam with a reasonable sea state and the harbour is sheltered.

g) It is best to avoid the overfalls off Start Point. The shallow water off the Skerries Bank is marked by a red buoy and will be to windward of the boat. Keep a good look-out for local fishing boats.

15.2

Leaving the mooring at about 0700 BST should be early enough to catch the tide and get to Torquay with favourable conditions.

The departure could be as early as 0600 but not later than about 0800 BST or the tide will have turned against the boat by the time it gets to Berry Head.

15.3

Fix at 0808 BST: 50°11'.65N 004°44'.3W

15.4

The yacht will pass 1.25 miles south of the lighthouse.

EP at 0908 BST: 50°12'.2N 004°36'.9W

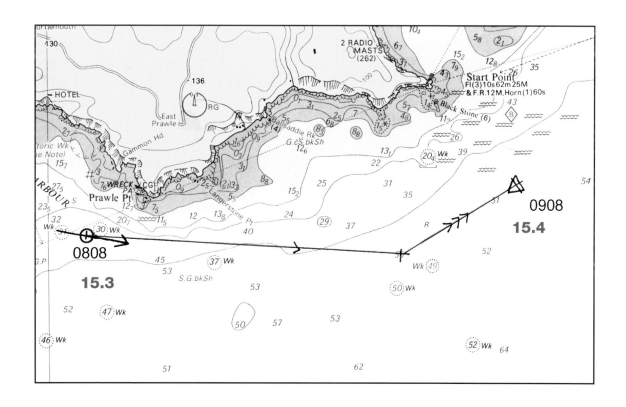

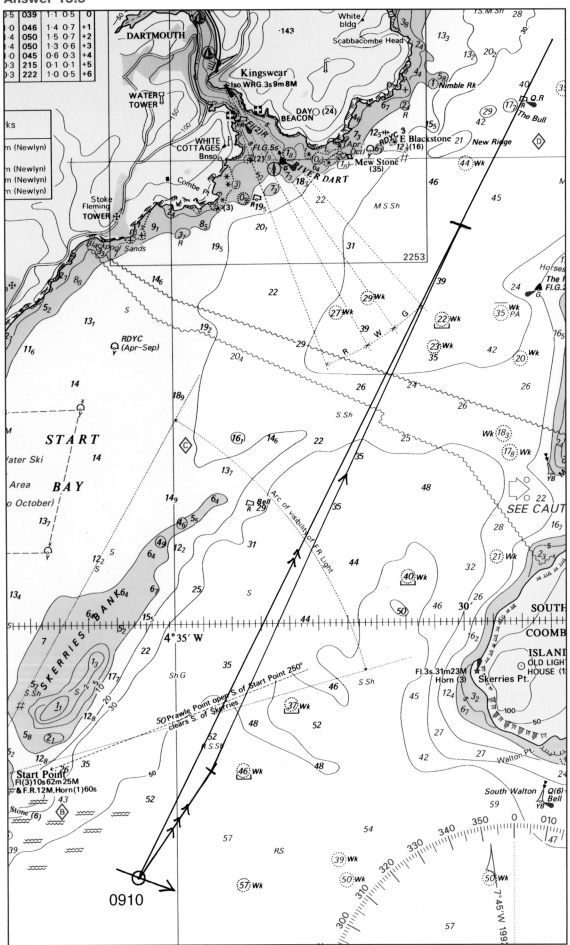

15.5

a) HW + 2 hours   035°(T)   1.4 knots.   Course to steer: 026°(T)   031°(M).

b) Leeway 10° so head up into the wind to 021°(M).

c) The yacht should be at the buoy at approximately 1020 BST.

d) The buoy will be sighted fine on the starboard bow.

Taking bearings of the buoy, which should remain constant, would make an easy check. The bearing should be the same as the ground track.

Alternatively the buoy could have been used as a waypoint and then the course checked against the cross track error.

15.6

1040 position 50°23'.05N   004°27'.0W

No. The direction and distance information that the GPS is giving is useful for plotting positions on the chart, quicker and more convenient than using the latitude and longitude display.

It is safe to alter course from this position but the direction displayed is not a course to steer, because the GPS has made no allowance for the tidal stream or leeway. Calculating a course to steer and using the GPS cross track error information for checking is a good working method.

Answer 15.6

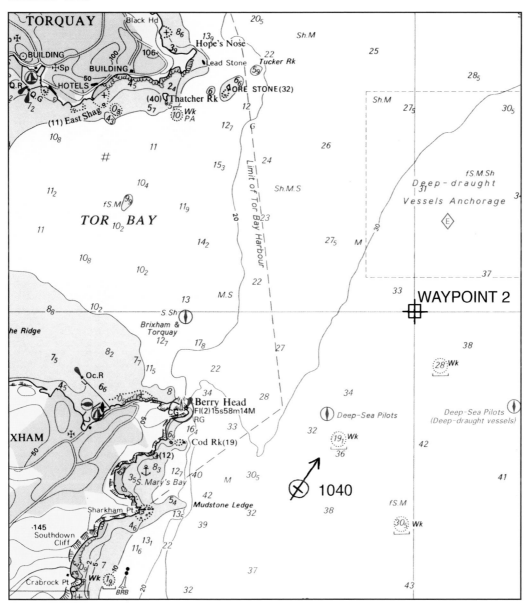

15.7

a) Height of tide at 1130 BST is 2.9m.

b) Least depth 1.5m, shown on the chartlet of Torquay Marina near main berths.

c) Depth of water near the pontoons at 1130 BST: Height of tide + charted depth: 2.9m +1.5m = 4.4m.

   Depth of water near the pontoons at LW: Charted depth + next LW: 1.5m + 0.5 = 2.0m.

15.8

a) Monday 13th May   HW   Saint Malo   1604
   Difference Carteret   + 31
   BST correction   nil (French standard time the
                                        same as BST)
   HW Carteret   1635 BST

   Access to the non-tidal marina for a vessel drawing 1.5m HW – 2$^{1}/_{2}$ to + 3 hours.

   Earliest time vessel can leave the marina: 1635 – 2$^{1}/_{2}$ hrs = 1405 BST.

b) HW Plymouth 1540 BST   mid range

   Yes. The tidal stream charts show favourable tidal streams from 1410 BST.

c) Yes. The distance from Carteret to the Alderney Race is approximately 25 miles.

   During the sail up to the race, the yacht will benefit from a tidal lift of more than six miles.

   Given a speed through the water of 6 knots, the vessel should be able to make the tidal gate with ease.

d) Working back from the Alderney Race:

   WTP 004:   1910 BST
   WTP 003:   1810 BST
   WTP 002:   1710 BST
   WTP 001:   1610 BST

   These times are based on a predicted SOG of about 7.0 knots.

15.9

Yes. After making the secondary port correction, HW Diellette (Flamanville) is found to be 1654 BST.

Access to the marina is until HW + 3 hrs: 1954 BST.

The flooding is discovered at 1740 BST, leaving 2$^{1}/_{4}$ hours to reach Diellette, which is just over four miles away.

15.10

a) Position: 49°41'.7N   005°09'.2W

b) Yes. The 1800 position is approximately $^{1}/_{2}$ mile away from waypoint 003, which has a target time of 1810. If the current progress continues, the yacht should reach the race at the planned time.

15.11

From 2010 BST the tidal stream charts show the tide flowing westward for the next six hours.

The yacht should set off on port tack, lee bowing the tide in order to make the best progress towards Plymouth.

15.12

a) Position: 50°01'.6N 005°05'.8W

b) ii) The yacht is between the shipping lanes, the traffic to the north is heading generally west.

15.13

Tuesday 14th May   HW   Plymouth 0402 BST   Range 3.5m

Distance to go 11.7 miles, boat speed 6.0 knots = two hour vector.

⟨C⟩ HW – 3   0032 – 0132 BST   279°(T)   1.7sp   0.8np   Int 1.3 knots

　　 HW – 2   0132 – 0232 BST   296°(T)   0.6sp   0.3np   Int 0.5 knots

a) Course to steer　　　332°(T)
　　Leeway　　　　　　　+ 5°
　　　　　　　　　　　　337°(T)
　　Variation　　　　　　+ 7° W
　　　　　　　　　　　　344°(M)
　　Deviation　　　　　　+ 5° W
　　　　　　　　　　　　<u>349°(C)</u>

b) SOG 6.6 knots   COG 327°(T)

c) $\dfrac{\text{Distance to go } 11.7M}{\text{SOG} \qquad 6.6kn}$ x 60 = 1hr 46mins

Extracts

INFORMATION CONTAINED IN THESE EXTRACTS MUST NOT BE USED FOR NAVIGATION.

The information is compiled from several nautical publications and the RYA Training Charts of a fictitious area.

Latitude and longitude have been removed from harbour plans because their actual positions differ from those shown on the RYA Training Charts.

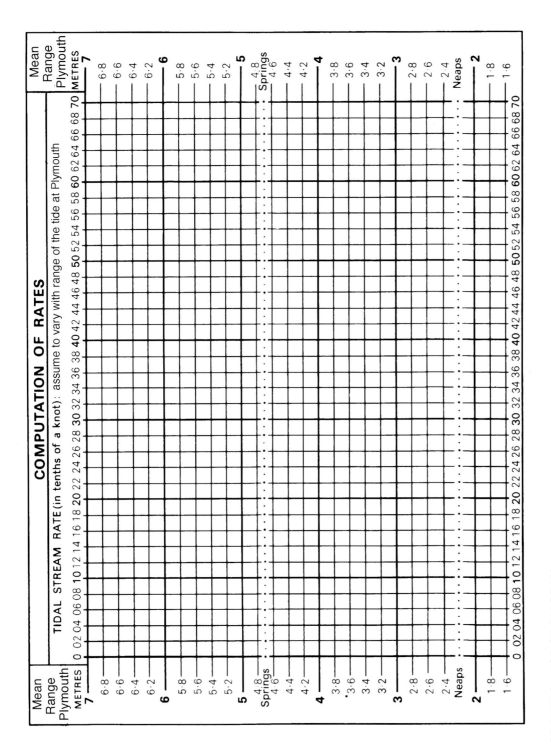

COMPUTATION OF RATES

TIDAL STREAM RATE (in tenths of a knot) : assume to vary with range of the tide at Plymouth

COMPUTATION OF RATES - USE OF DIAGRAM

Example to predict the rate of tidal stream at 0756 BST on Friday 7 June
in the Alderney Race using the data from the tidal stream atlas.
From Plymouth tide table (page 24).
LW 0440 (BST) 0.9m ⎱
 ⎰ **Range 4.1m**
HW 1056 (BST) 5.0m

From the tidal stream atlas (page 6). 0756 (BST) = 3 hours before HW Plymouth.
The rates in the Alderney Race would be **2.3kn** (neaps) **5.7kn** (springs).

Using the computation of rates table: -
(1) Where the dotted neaps line intersects **2.3kn** make a small circle around the dot.
(2) Where the dotted springs line intersects **5.7kn** make a small circle around the dot.
(3) Join these marks with a straight line.
(4) Draw a horizontal line from **4.1m** (the morning range) until it intersects the line drawn in step 3.
(5) From this intersection draw a vertical line, up or down, and note the tidal stream rate, in this
example **4.9kn.**

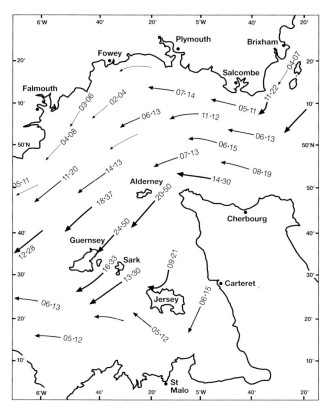

**5 hours before HW Plymouth
(2 hours after HW Dover)**

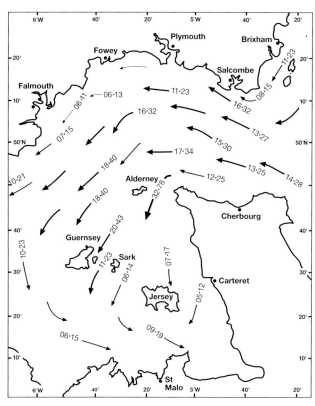

**4 hours before HW Plymouth
(3 hours after HW Dover)**

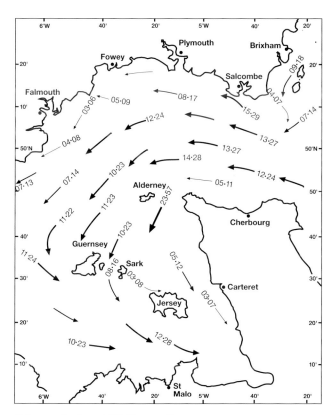

**3 hours before HW Plymouth
(4 hours after HW Dover)**

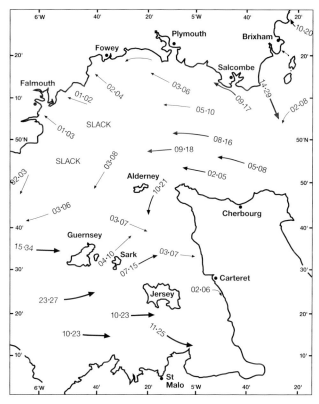

**2 hours before HW Plymouth
(5 hours after HW Dover)**

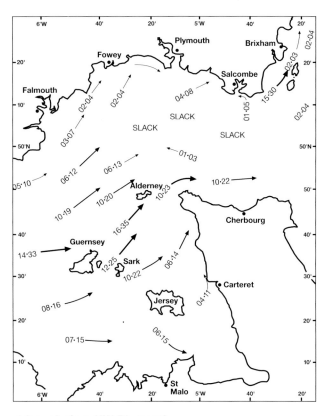

**1 hour before HW Plymouth
(6 hours after HW Dover)**

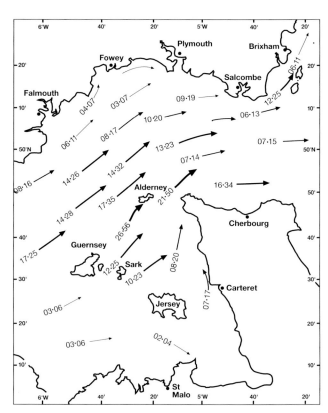

**HW Plymouth
(5 hours before HW Dover)**

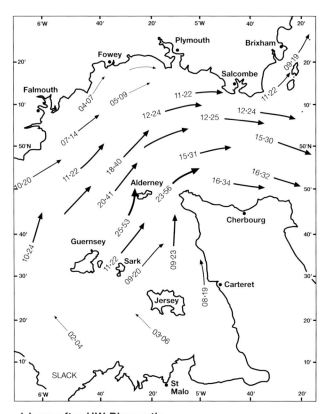

**1 hour after HW Plymouth
(4 hours before HW Dover)**

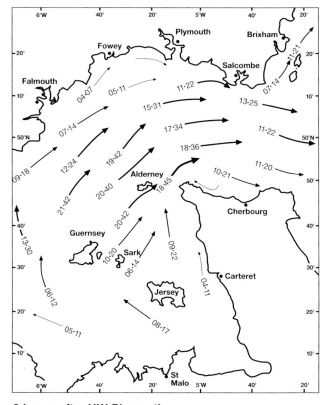

**2 hours after HW Plymouth
(3 hours before HW Dover)**

TIDAL STREAM CHARTS

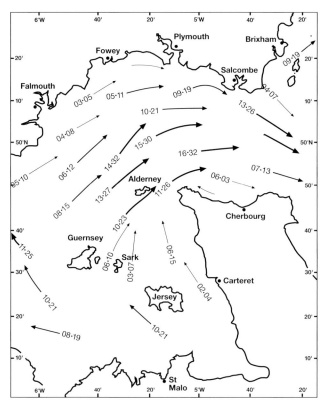

3 hours after HW Plymouth
(2 hours before HW Dover)

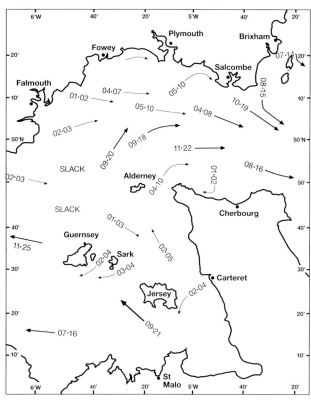

4 hours after HW Plymouth
(1 hour before HW Dover)

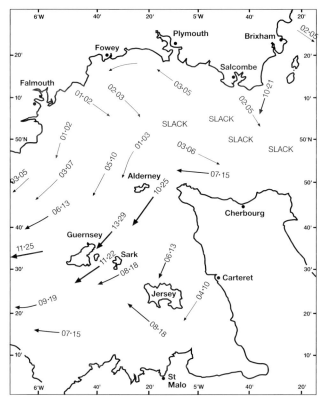

5 hours after HW Plymouth
(HW Dover)

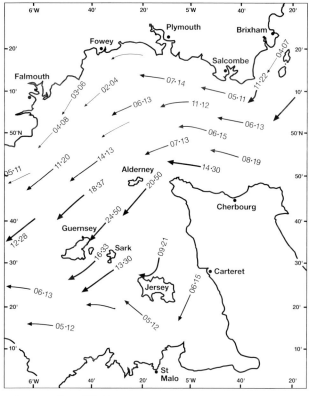

6 hours after HW Plymouth
(1 hour after HW Dover)

FOWEY

CHARTS
AC 31, 148, *1267*; Imray C6, Y52; Stanfords 13; OS 204

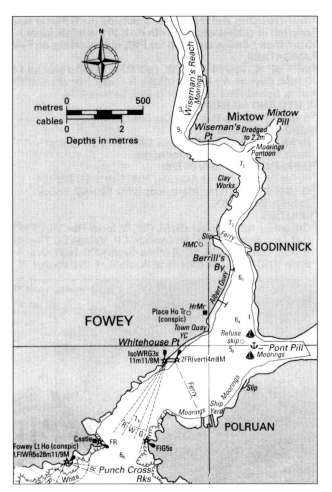

Standard Port PLYMOUTH (→)

Times				Height (metres)			
High Water		Low Water		MHWS	MHWN	MLWN	MLWS
0000	0600	0000	0600	5.5	4.4	2.2	0.8
1200	1800	1200	1800				
Differences FOWEY							
-0010	-0015	-0010	-0005	-0.1	-0.1	-0.2	-0.2
LOSTWITHIEL							
+0005	-0010	Dries		-4.1	-4.1	Dries	
PAR							
-0005	-0015	0000	-0010	-0.4	-0.4	-0.4	-0.2

SHELTER
Good, but exposed to winds from S to SW. Gales from these directions can cause heavy swell in the lower hbr and confused seas, especially on the ebb. Entry at any tide in any conditions. Speed limit 6kn. All visitors buoys are White and marked 'FHC VISITORS'.

NAVIGATION
207°/027° from/to Whitehouse Pt It, Iso WRG 3s. Appr in W sector of Fowey It ho. W sector of Whitehouse Pt It leads 027° through hbr ent. 3M E of ent beware Udder Rk marked by unlit SCM buoy. From SW beware Cannis Rk (4ca SE of Gribbin Hd) with SCM buoy, Q (6) + L Fl 15s. Entering hbr, keep well clear of Punch Cross Rks to stbd. Caution: Fowey is a busy commercial clay port. Unmarked chan is navigable up to Golant, but moorings restrict anchoring space. Lerryn (1.6M) and Lostwithiel (3M) are accessible on the tide by shoal draft.

LIGHTS AND MARKS
An unlt RWtr 33m on Gribbin Hd (1.3M WSW of hbr ent) is conspic from all sea directions, as is a white house 3ca E of hbr ent. Lt ho is conspic, L Fl WR 5s 28m 11/9M, R284°-295°, W295°-028°, R028°-054°. Whitehouse Pt Iso WRG 3s 11m 11/8M. G017°-022°. W022°-032°, R032°-037°. Ent is marked by Lamp Rk SHM bn Fl G 5s 7m 2M, vis 088°-205°, and St Catherine's Pt FR 15m 2M, vis 150°-295°.

RADIO TELEPHONE
Call *Fowey* Hbr Radio Ch 12 09 16 (HO). Hbr Patrol (0900-2000LT) Ch 12 16. *Fowey Relueller* Ch 10 16. Water taxi Ch 06. Pilots Ch 09. Tugs Ch 09 12.

FACILITIES
Albert Quay Pontoon L, FW; **Polruan Quay** Slip, P, D, L, FW, C (3 ton); **Royal Fowey YC**, FW, Showers, R, Bar; **Fowey Gallants** SC 832335, Showers, Bar; **Fowey Refueller** (0900-1800LT daily; winter Mon-Fri) VHF Ch 10, 16, D. **Services:** M, FW, Gas, Gaz, CH, ACA.

LOOE

CHARTS
AC 147, 146, 1267; Imray C6; Stanfords 13; OS 201

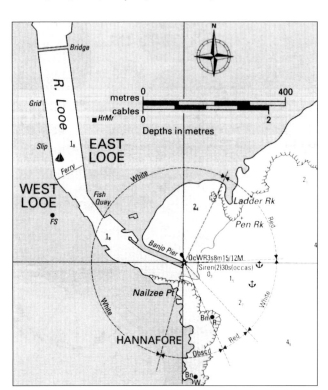

Standard Port PLYMOUTH (→)

Times				Height (metres)			
High Water		Low Water		MHWS	MHWN	MLWN	MLWS
0000	0600	0000	0600	5.5	4.4	2.2	0.8
1200	1800	1200	1800				
Differences LOOE							
-0010	-0010	-0005	-0005	-0.1	-0.2	-0.2	-0.2
WHITSAND BAY							
0000	0000	0000	0000	0.0	+0.1	-0.1	+0.2

SHELTER
Good, but uncomfortable in strong SE winds.anchorage in 2m E of the pier hd; access approx HW ±1¹/2h. visitors berth, above ferry, is marked in Y on W side of hbr which dries 2.4m to the ent. The W bank has rky outcrops to S of ferry.

NAVIGATION
130°/310° from/to pier hd It. Ent dangerous in strong SE'lies, when seas break heavily on the bar. From W, beware The Ranneys, rks 2ca SE of Looe Is. Do not attempt the rky passage between Looe Is and mainland except with local knowledge and at HW. From E, beware Longstone Rks extending 1¹/2ca from shore NE of hbr ent. At sp, ebb tide runs up to 5kn.

LIGHTS AND MARKS
Looe Island (or St George's Is) is conspic (44m), 8ca S of the ent. Mid Main bn (off Hannafore Pt, halfway between pier hd and Looe Is) Q (3) 10s 2M; ECM. At night appr in W sector (267°-313°) of pier hd It Oc WR 3s 8m 15/12M; vis W013° 207°, R207° 267°, W267° 313°, R313 332; siren (2) 30s, fishing. No Its inside hbr.

RADIO TELEPHONE VHF Ch 16 (occas).

TELEPHONE (Dial code 01503)
Hr Mr 262839; CG 262138; MRSC (01803) 882704; Marinecall 0891 500458; Police 262233; Dr 263195.

FACILITIES
W Looe Quay AB £11.28, Slip, M, P & D (cans), L, FW, ME, El, CH; **E Looe Quay** Access HW ±3, Slip, P & D (cans), L, FW, ME, El, C (2¹/2 ton); Looe SC 262559, L, R, Bar. **Services:** Sh (Wood), Sh, Gas.

CHARTS
AC *871*, 1902, 1901, *9219*, 1967, 1900, *1267*, 1613; Imray C14; Stanfords 13; OS 201

Standard Port PLYMOUTH (→)

Times				Height (metres)			
High Water		Low Water		MHWS	MHWN	MLWN	MLWS
0000	0600	0000	0600	5.5	4.4	2.2	0.8
1200	1800	1200	1800				
Differences BOVISAND PIER							
0000	-0020	0000	-0010	-0.2	-0.1	0.0	+0.1
TURNCHAPEL (Cattewater)							
0000	0000	+0010	-0015	0.0	+0.1	+0.2	+0.1
JUPITER POINT (R. Lynher)							
+0010	+0005	0000	-0005	0.0	0.0	+0.1	0.0
ST GERMANS (R. Lynher)							
0000	0000	+0020	+0020	-0.3	-0.1	0.0	+0.2
SALTASH (R. Tamar)							
0000	+0010	0000	-0005	+0.1	+0.1	+0.1	+0.1
CARGREEN (R. Tamar)							
0000	+0010	+0020	+0020	0.0	0.0	-0.1	0.0
COTEHELE QUAY (R. Tamar)							
0000	+0020	+0045	+0045	-0.9	-0.9	-0.8	-0.4

NOTE: Devonpont is a Standard Port; Winds from SE to W increase the flood and retard the ebb; vice versa in winds from the NW to E.

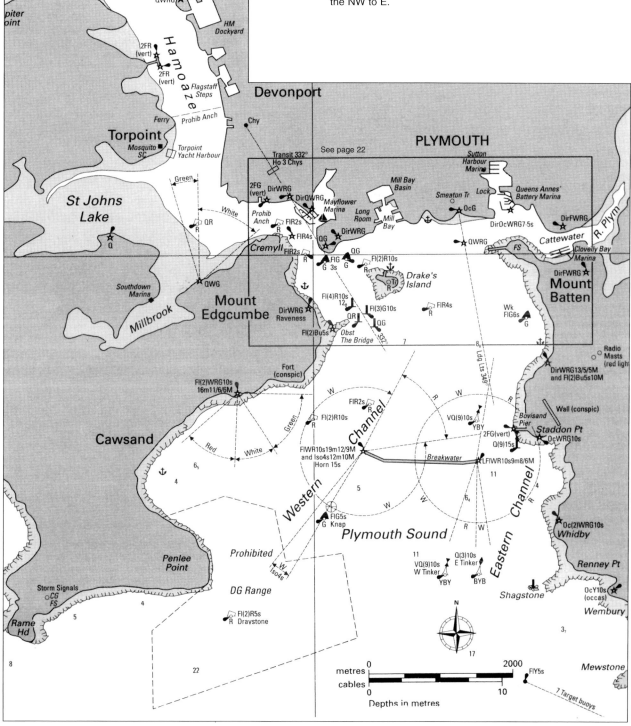

See page 22

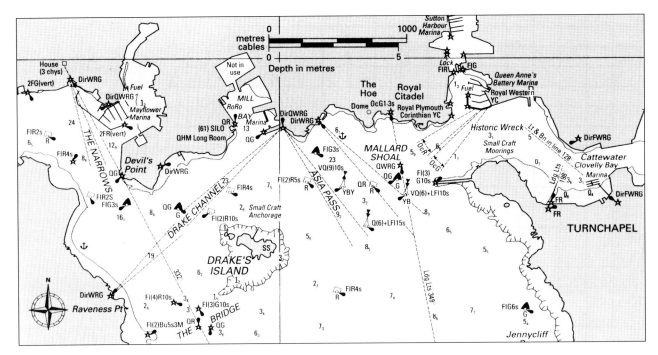

SHELTER

Excellent. Plymouth is a Naval Base, a busy commercial/ferry port principally using Mill Bay Docks, and an active fishing port based mainly on Sutton Harbour which is entered via a lock (see Facilities). There are marinas to E and W of the city centre, as well as in the Cattewater, off Torpoint and in Millbrook Lake. Around the Sound there are anchorages, sheltered according to the wind, in Cawsand Bay, in Barn Pool (below Mt Edgcumbe), N of Drake's Is, below The Hoe and in Jennycliff Bay to the E. Also good shelter W of Cremyll and off the Hamoaze in the R Lynher and in the R Tamar/Tavy above Saltash.

NAVIGATION

213°/033° from/toW bkwtr It. The Sound can be entered via the W or E Chans which are well lit/buoyed with no real hazards. There are no shoal patches with less than 3.7m at MLWS. Yachts need not keep to the deep water chans.

The short cut to the Hamoaze via The Bridge (channel between Drake's Is and Mt Edgcumbe) is lit by 2 PHM and 2 SHM bns; the seaward pair show QR and QG, the inner pair Fl (4) R 10s and Fl (3) G 10s. The QR bn and the Fl (4) R 10s bn both have tide gauges calibrated to show height of tide above CD; charted depth is 2.lm. The E'ly of 3 conspic high-rise blocks brg 331° leads through The Bridge chan. Caution: a charted depth 1.8m is close SW of No 3 SHM bn, Fl (3) G 10s.

Speed limits: l0kn N of The Breakwater, 8kn in Cattewater (where outbound vessels have right of way), 4kn in Sutton Chan and 5kn in Sutton Hbr.

LIGHTS AND MARKS

Bkwtr W hd, Fl WR l0s 19m 12/9M (vis W262°-208°, R208°-262°) and Iso 4s 12m l0M (vis 033°-037°). Bkwtr E hd, L Fl WR l0s 9m 8/6M (R190°-353°, W353°-001°, R001°-018°, W018°-190°). Mallard Shoal ldg Its 349°: Front Q WRG 10/3M (vis G233°-043°, R043°-067°, G067°-087°, W087°-099°, R099°-108°); rear 396m from front (on Hoe) Oc G 1.3s (vis 310°-040°). There are Dir WRG Its, all lit H24 except **,at Whidbey (138.5°), Staddon Pt (044'), Withyhedge (070°), W Hoe bn (315°), Western King (271°), Mill Bay** (048.5°), Ravenness (225°), Mount Wise (343°), and Ocean Court** (085°). In fog the following Dir W Its operate: Mallard (front) Fl 5s (vis 232°-110°); West Hoe bn F (vis 313°-317°); Eastern King Fl 5s (vis 259°-062°); Ravenness Fl (2)15s (vis 160°- 305°); Mount Wise F (vis 341°-345°); Ocean Court Fl 5s (vis 270°-100°).

Notes: Principal Its in Plymouth Sound show QY if mains power fails. N of The Bkwtr, four large mooring buoys (C, D, E & F) have Fl Y Its.

BYELAWS/NAVAL ACTIVITY

The whole Port is under the jurisdiction of the QHM, but certain areas are locally controlled, i.e. by Cattewater Commissioners and by ABP who operate Mill Bay Docks. Beware frequent movements of naval vessels, which have right of way in the chans. Obey MOD Police orders. Info on Naval activities may be obtained from Naval Ops.

RADIO TELEPHONE

Call: *Long Room Port Control* VHF Ch 08 12 **14** 16 (H24). *Mill Bay Docks* Ch 12 13 14 16 (only during ferry ops). *Sutton Lock*, for lock opening and marina, Ch **12** 16 (H24). *Cattewater Hbr* Ch 14 16 (Mon-Fri, 0900-1700LT). Maytlower, Queen Anne's Battery, Sutton Hbr & Clovelly Bay marinas and Torpoint Yacht Hbr: all Ch **80** M.

FACILITIES

Marinas (W to E)

Torpoint Yacht Hbr (60+20 visitors) £10, access H24, dredged 2m. FW, AC, BY, C, ME, El, Sh, Diver, SM.

Southdown Marina (35 inc visitors) £7.50, access HW±4; AB on pontoon (2m) or on drying quay; FW, AC, D.

Mayflower Marina (300+50 visitors) £18.20 inc AC, P, D, FW, ME, El, Sh, C (2 ton), BH (25 ton), CH, Slip, Gas, Gaz, Divers, SM, BY, YC, V, R, Bar.

Mill Bay Village Marina, VHF Ch M. NO VISITORS. Ent Its = Oc R 4s & Oc G 4s, not on chartlet

Queen Anne's Battery Marina (240+60 visitors) £16.10, AC, P, D, ME, El, Sh, FW, BH (20 ton), C (50 ton), CH, Gas, Gaz, SM, Slip, V, Bar, YC.

Sutton Hbr Marina (310), £15, P, D, FW, AC, El, ME, Sh, CH, C (masts only), Slip. Sutton Hbr is entered via lock (Barbican flood protection scheme), which maintains 3m CD in the marina. Lock (floating fenders) operates H24, free; call *Sutton Lock* VHF Ch 12 16. When tide reaches 3m CD, gates stay open for free-low. Tfc Its (vert): 3 ® = Stop; 3 G = Go; 3 Fl R = Serious hazard, wait.

Clovelly Bay Marina (180+ visitors), £14.48, D, FW, AC, CH, ME, El, Gas, Gaz, V.

Signal	Meaning
Unlit	No restrictions, unless passed on VHF
® ® All Fl ®	Serious Emergency All traffic suspended
® Ⓖ All Oc Ⓖ	Outgoing traffic only may proceed on the recommended track. Crossing traffic to seek approval from Port Control*
Ⓖ Ⓖ All Oc ®	Incoming traffic only may proceed on the recommended track. Crossing traffic to seek approval from Port Control*
Ⓖ Ⓖ All Oc Ⓦ	Vessels may proceed in either direction, but shall give a wide berth to HM Ships using the recommended track

*Call Port Control Ch 13 or 14, but craft <20m LOA may proceed in the contrary direction, with care and not impeding the passage of vessels for which the signal is intended.

ENGLAND - PLYMOUTH (DEVONPORT)

TIME ZONE (UT)
For Summer Time add ONE hour in non-shaded areas

TIMES AND HEIGHTS OF HIGH AND LOW WATERS

JANUARY

Day	Time	m		Day	Time	m
1 M	0202 / 0821 / 1429 / 2054	4.5 / 2.1 / 4.5 / 1.9		**16** TU	0043 / 0715 / 1316 / 1957	4.5 / 2.0 / 4.6 / 1.8
2 TU	0302 / 0925 / 1526 / 2149	4.7 / 1.9 / 4.7 / 1.7		**17** W	0206 / 0835 / 1440 / 2110	4.7 / 1.7 / 4.8 / 1.5
3 W	0352 / 1016 / 1615 / 2236	4.9 / 1.6 / 4.8 / 1.5		**18** TH	0321 / 0944 / 1551 / 2214	5.0 / 1.3 / 5.0 / 1.2
4 TH	0435 / 1101 / 1656 / 2317	5.1 / 1.4 / 5.0 / 1.3		**19** F	0422 / 1045 / 1651 / 2310	5.3 / 0.9 / 5.3 / 0.8
5 F O	0513 / 1141 / 1733 / 2354	5.2 / 1.2 / 5.0 / 1.2		**20** SA ●	0515 / 1139 / 1744	5.6 / 0.6 / 5.4
6 SA	0549 / 1217 / 1810	5.3 / 1.2 / 5.1		**21** SU	0003 / 0606 / 1231 / 1835	0.5 / 5.8 / 0.3 / 5.5
7 SU	0028 / 0626 / 1251 / 1848	1.2 / 5.3 / 1.1 / 5.1		**22** M	0052 / 0657 / 1319 / 1926	0.4 / 5.8 / 0.2 / 5.6
8 M	0059 / 0703 / 1321 / 1926	1.2 / 5.3 / 1.2 / 5.0		**23** TU	0138 / 0745 / 1403 / 2012	0.3 / 5.8 / 0.2 / 5.5
9 TU	0129 / 0740 / 1351 / 2002	1.2 / 5.2 / 1.2 / 5.0		**24** W	0220 / 0828 / 1444 / 2054	0.4 / 5.7 / 0.4 / 5.4
10 W	0159 / 0814 / 1419 / 2034	1.3 / 5.2 / 1.3 / 4.9		**25** TH	0259 / 0911 / 1522 / 2132	0.7 / 5.5 / 0.7 / 5.2
11 TH	0228 / 0845 / 1449 / 2104	1.4 / 5.1 / 1.4 / 4.8		**26** F	0336 / 0948 / 1559 / 2207	1.0 / 5.2 / 1.2 / 4.9
12 F	0301 / 0918 / 1523 / 2140	1.5 / 4.9 / 1.5 / 4.7		**27** SA	0414 / 1023 / 1638 / 2243	1.4 / 4.9 / 1.6 / 4.6
13 SA	0340 / 0959 / 1606 / 2227	1.7 / 4.8 / 1.7 / 4.6		**28** SU	0458 / 1104 / 1726 / 2337	1.8 / 4.5 / 2.0 / 4.4
14 SU	0430 / 1052 / 1705 / 2329	1.9 / 4.7 / 1.9 / 4.5		**29** M	0555 / 1218 / 1829	2.2 / 4.3 / 2.2
15 M	0543 / 1158 / 1831	2.0 / 4.6 / 2.0		**30** TU	0107 / 0712 / 1348 / 1956	4.3 / 2.3 / 4.2 / 2.3
				31 W	0223 / 0848 / 1455 / 2117	4.4 / 2.2 / 4.4 / 2.0

FEBRUARY

Day	Time	m		Day	Time	m
1 TH	0322 / 0951 / 1549 / 2211	4.6 / 1.8 / 4.6 / 1.7		**16** F	0301 / 0930 / 1538 / 2201	4.9 / 1.4 / 4.9 / 1.2
2 F	0409 / 1039 / 1633 / 2255	4.9 / 1.5 / 4.8 / 1.4		**17** SA	0406 / 1033 / 1638 / 2259	5.2 / 0.9 / 5.2 / 0.8
3 SA	0450 / 1120 / 1713 / 2334	5.1 / 1.3 / 5.0 / 1.2		**18** SU ●	0501 / 1127 / 1731 / 2349	5.5 / 0.5 / 5.4 / 0.5
4 SU O	0529 / 1157 / 1752	5.2 / 1.1 / 5.1		**19** M	0551 / 1216 / 1820	5.7 / 0.2 / 5.5
5 M	0009 / 0608 / 1232 / 1831	1.1 / 5.3 / 1.0 / 5.1		**20** TU	0036 / 0639 / 1301 / 1907	0.2 / 5.8 / 0.1 / 5.6
6 TU	0042 / 0647 / 1304 / 1910	1.0 / 5.3 / 0.9 / 5.1		**21** W	0119 / 0726 / 1343 / 1950	0.2 / 5.8 / 0.1 / 5.6
7 W	0113 / 0725 / 1333 / 1945	1.0 / 5.3 / 0.9 / 5.1		**22** TH	0159 / 0808 / 1421 / 2027	0.3 / 5.7 / 0.3 / 5.4
8 TH	0142 / 0758 / 1402 / 2016	1.0 / 5.2 / 1.0 / 5.0		**23** F	0235 / 0844 / 1455 / 2057	0.5 / 5.5 / 0.7 / 5.2
9 F	0212 / 0828 / 1431 / 2044	1.0 / 5.2 / 1.1 / 5.0		**24** SA	0308 / 0912 / 1527 / 2121	0.9 / 5.2 / 1.1 / 5.0
10 SA	0243 / 0858 / 1503 / 2116	1.1 / 5.1 / 1.2 / 4.9		**25** SU	0341 / 0936 / 1600 / 2149	1.3 / 4.8 / 1.5 / 4.7
11 SU	0319 / 0935 / 1541 / 2158	1.3 / 4.9 / 1.4 / 4.7		**26** M	0418 / 1008 / 1640 / 2231	1.7 / 4.5 / 2.0 / 4.4
12 M	0403 / 1024 / 1630 / 2255	1.6 / 4.7 / 1.7 / 4.6		**27** TU	0507 / 1059 / 1737 / 2336	2.1 / 4.2 / 2.3 / 4.2
13 TU	0505 / 1129 / 1744	1.9 / 4.5 / 1.9		**28** W	0617 / 1241 / 1853	2.4 / 4.0 / 2.4
14 W	0010 / 0637 / 1251 / 1926	4.5 / 2.0 / 4.4 / 2.0				
15 TH	0139 / 0813 / 1421 / 2053	4.6 / 1.8 / 4.6 / 1.7				

MARCH

Day	Time	m		Day	Time	m
1 F	0248 / 0918 / 1521 / 2140	4.4 / 2.0 / 4.4 / 1.9		**16** SA	0245 / 0917 / 1526 / 2148	4.8 / 1.4 / 4.8 / 1.3
2 SA	0341 / 1011 / 1608 / 2227	4.7 / 1.6 / 4.7 / 1.5		**17** SU	0350 / 1018 / 1624 / 2243	5.2 / 0.9 / 5.1 / 0.8
3 SU	0425 / 1052 / 1650 / 2307	5.0 / 1.3 / 4.9 / 1.2		**18** M	0443 / 1109 / 1714 / 2331	5.5 / 0.5 / 5.4 / 0.5
4 M	0506 / 1130 / 1730 / 2344	5.2 / 1.0 / 5.1 / 1.0		**19** TU ●	0532 / 1156 / 1800	5.6 / 0.3 / 5.5
5 TU O	0546 / 1206 / 1810	5.3 / 0.9 / 5.2		**20** W	0016 / 0618 / 1239 / 1842	0.3 / 5.7 / 0.1 / 5.6
6 W	0019 / 0625 / 1240 / 1848	0.8 / 5.3 / 0.8 / 5.2		**21** TH	0057 / 0702 / 1319 / 1922	0.2 / 5.7 / 0.2 / 5.5
7 TH	0052 / 0703 / 1312 / 1924	0.8 / 5.3 / 0.7 / 5.2		**22** F	0135 / 0741 / 1355 / 1955	0.3 / 5.6 / 0.4 / 5.4
8 F	0123 / 0738 / 1342 / 1955	0.8 / 5.3 / 0.8 / 5.2		**23** SA	0209 / 0813 / 1427 / 2020	0.5 / 5.4 / 0.7 / 5.2
9 SA	0154 / 0810 / 1413 / 2024	0.8 / 5.2 / 0.9 / 5.1		**24** SU	0241 / 0837 / 1457 / 2043	0.9 / 5.1 / 1.1 / 5.0
10 SU	0227 / 0842 / 1445 / 2057	0.9 / 5.1 / 1.0 / 5.0		**25** M	0311 / 0901 / 1527 / 2113	1.3 / 4.8 / 1.5 / 4.8
11 M	0303 / 0920 / 1523 / 2139	1.1 / 4.9 / 1.3 / 4.8		**26** TU	0344 / 0935 / 1602 / 2153	1.7 / 4.5 / 1.9 / 4.5
12 TU	0347 / 1008 / 1612 / 2234	1.4 / 4.7 / 1.6 / 4.6		**27** W	0429 / 1022 / 1655 / 2249	2.1 / 4.2 / 2.3 / 4.3
13 W	0447 / 1113 / 1722 / 2349	1.8 / 4.5 / 1.9 / 4.5		**28** TH	0536 / 1134 / 1810	2.3 / 4.0 / 2.4
14 TH	0616 / 1238 / 1906	1.9 / 4.4 / 2.0		**29** F	0016 / 0654 / 1337 / 1928	4.2 / 2.3 / 4.1 / 2.3
15 F	0121 / 0758 / 1410 / 2039	4.5 / 1.8 / 4.5 / 1.7		**30** SA	0204 / 0816 / 1446 / 2047	4.3 / 2.1 / 4.3 / 2.0
				31 SU	0305 / 0924 / 1537 / 2146	4.6 / 1.7 / 4.6 / 1.6

APRIL

Day	Time	m		Day	Time	m
1 M	0354 / 1013 / 1621 / 2231	4.9 / 1.3 / 4.9 / 1.3		**16** TU	0422 / 1047 / 1651 / 2309	5.3 / 0.6 / 5.3 / 0.6
2 TU	0437 / 1054 / 1703 / 2312	5.1 / 1.1 / 5.1 / 1.0		**17** W	0509 / 1132 / 1735 / 2353 ●	5.5 / 0.4 / 5.4 / 0.4
3 W	0519 / 1134 / 1743 / 2351	5.3 / 0.8 / 5.2 / 0.8		**18** TH	0554 / 1214 / 1816	5.5 / 0.4 / 5.5
4 TH O	0559 / 1211 / 1822	5.3 / 0.7 / 5.3		**19** F	0033 / 0635 / 1253 / 1852	0.4 / 5.5 / 0.5 / 5.4
5 F	0028 / 0638 / 1248 / 1858	0.7 / 5.4 / 0.6 / 5.3		**20** SA	0110 / 0712 / 1328 / 1923	0.5 / 5.4 / 0.6 / 5.4
6 SA	0104 / 0716 / 1323 / 1933	0.6 / 5.4 / 0.7 / 5.3		**21** SU	0144 / 0742 / 1400 / 1948	0.7 / 5.2 / 0.9 / 5.3
7 SU	0139 / 0753 / 1357 / 2008	0.7 / 5.3 / 0.8 / 5.3		**22** M	0215 / 0807 / 1430 / 2015	1.0 / 5.0 / 1.2 / 5.1
8 M	0215 / 0831 / 1434 / 2045	0.8 / 5.2 / 1.0 / 5.2		**23** TU	0246 / 0836 / 1459 / 2048	1.3 / 4.8 / 1.5 / 4.9
9 TU	0254 / 0912 / 1514 / 2128	1.0 / 5.0 / 1.3 / 5.0		**24** W	0317 / 0912 / 1531 / 2127	1.6 / 4.6 / 1.9 / 4.7
10 W	0341 / 1002 / 1605 / 2223	1.3 / 4.7 / 1.6 / 4.8		**25** TH	0357 / 0957 / 1617 / 2216	1.9 / 4.3 / 2.1 / 4.4
11 TH	0441 / 1107 / 1715 / 2337	1.6 / 4.5 / 1.9 / 4.6		**26** F	0458 / 1058 / 1728 / 2323	2.2 / 4.1 / 2.3 / 4.3
12 F	0606 / 1231 / 1851	1.8 / 4.4 / 2.0		**27** SA	0612 / 1228 / 1843	2.2 / 4.1 / 2.3
13 SA	0107 / 0741 / 1357 / 2020	4.6 / 1.7 / 4.5 / 1.7		**28** SU	0054 / 0722 / 1356 / 1951	4.3 / 2.1 / 4.3 / 2.1
14 SU	0225 / 0857 / 1507 / 2127	4.8 / 1.4 / 4.8 / 1.3		**29** M	0215 / 0826 / 1456 / 2054	4.5 / 1.8 / 4.6 / 1.7
15 M	0329 / 0956 / 1603 / 2222	5.1 / 1.0 / 5.1 / 0.9		**30** TU	0313 / 0924 / 1545 / 2148	4.8 / 1.4 / 4.8 / 1.4

Chart Datum: 3·22 metres below Ordnance Datum (Newlyn)

ENGLAND - PLYMOUTH (DEVONPORT)

TIME ZONE (UT)
For Summer Time add ONE hour in non-shaded areas

TIMES AND HEIGHTS OF HIGH AND LOW WATERS

MAY

Day	Time	m	Day	Time	m
1 W	0402 / 1014 / 1630 / 2236	5.0 / 1.1 / 5.1 / 1.1	16 TH	0445 / 1107 / 1709 / 2328	5.2 / 0.8 / 5.3 / 0.8
2 TH	0447 / 1059 / 1713 / 2321	5.2 / 0.9 / 5.2 / 0.8	17 F ●	0528 / 1149 / 1748	5.3 / 0.7 / 5.3
3 F O	0530 / 1143 / 1754	5.3 / 0.7 / 5.4	18 SA	0009 / 0608 / 1228 / 1823	0.7 / 5.2 / 0.8 / 5.3
4 SA	0003 / 0613 / 1225 / 1834	0.7 / 5.4 / 0.6 / 5.4	19 SU	0047 / 0644 / 1304 / 1854	0.8 / 5.2 / 0.9 / 5.3
5 SU	0046 / 0655 / 1306 / 1914	0.6 / 5.4 / 0.6 / 5.5	20 M	0122 / 0716 / 1336 / 1923	0.9 / 5.1 / 1.1 / 5.2
6 M	0127 / 0738 / 1347 / 1955	0.6 / 5.3 / 0.7 / 5.4	21 TU	0153 / 0746 / 1406 / 1955	1.1 / 4.9 / 1.3 / 5.1
7 TU	0209 / 0822 / 1429 / 2038	0.7 / 5.2 / 0.9 / 5.3	22 W	0224 / 0819 / 1436 / 2029	1.3 / 4.8 / 1.5 / 5.0
8 W	0252 / 0909 / 1513 / 2124	0.9 / 5.0 / 1.2 / 5.2	23 TH	0255 / 0856 / 1507 / 2107	1.5 / 4.6 / 1.7 / 4.8
9 TH	0342 / 1000 / 1605 / 2218	1.2 / 4.8 / 1.4 / 4.9	24 F	0330 / 0937 / 1544 / 2150	1.7 / 4.5 / 1.9 / 4.6
10 F	0440 / 1103 / 1709 / 2327	1.4 / 4.6 / 1.7 / 4.7	25 SA	0417 / 1028 / 1640 / 2242	1.9 / 4.3 / 2.1 / 4.5
11 SA	0554 / 1219 / 1829	1.6 / 4.5 / 1.8	26 SU	0524 / 1131 / 1754 / 2348	2.0 / 4.2 / 2.2 / 4.4
12 SU	0047 / 0715 / 1334 / 1950	4.7 / 1.6 / 4.6 / 1.7	27 M	0634 / 1247 / 1903	2.0 / 4.3 / 2.1
13 M	0200 / 0828 / 1440 / 2058	4.8 / 1.4 / 4.8 / 1.4	28 TU	0105 / 0738 / 1400 / 2007	4.5 / 1.8 / 4.5 / 1.8
14 TU	0302 / 0929 / 1536 / 2155	4.9 / 1.2 / 5.0 / 1.2	29 W	0219 / 0838 / 1501 / 2107	4.6 / 1.5 / 4.7 / 1.5
15 W	0357 / 1021 / 1625 / 2244	5.1 / 0.9 / 5.1 / 0.9	30 TH	0320 / 0935 / 1553 / 2202	4.9 / 1.2 / 5.0 / 1.2
			31 F	0413 / 1027 / 1641 / 2253	5.1 / 1.0 / 5.2 / 0.9

JUNE

Day	Time	m	Day	Time	m
1 SA O	0502 / 1117 / 1727 / 2342	5.2 / 0.8 / 5.4 / 0.7	16 SU ●	0543 / 1205 / 1757	5.0 / 1.0 / 5.2
2 SU	0550 / 1205 / 1812	5.3 / 0.6 / 5.5	17 M	0026 / 0619 / 1242 / 1831	1.0 / 5.0 / 1.0 / 5.2
3 M	0030 / 0638 / 1253 / 1858	0.5 / 5.4 / 0.6 / 5.6	18 TU	0102 / 0654 / 1315 / 1905	1.0 / 5.0 / 1.1 / 5.2
4 TU	0118 / 0726 / 1340 / 1945	0.5 / 5.4 / 0.6 / 5.6	19 W	0134 / 0729 / 1346 / 1939	1.1 / 4.9 / 1.2 / 5.1
5 W	0205 / 0815 / 1426 / 2032	0.5 / 5.3 / 0.7 / 5.5	20 TH	0205 / 0805 / 1416 / 2015	1.2 / 4.8 / 1.4 / 5.0
6 TH	0252 / 0904 / 1513 / 2119	0.7 / 5.2 / 0.9 / 5.3	21 F	0235 / 0842 / 1445 / 2050	1.4 / 4.7 / 1.5 / 4.9
7 F	0340 / 0956 / 1601 / 2211	0.9 / 5.0 / 1.2 / 5.1	22 SA	0305 / 0918 / 1516 / 2126	1.5 / 4.6 / 1.7 / 4.8
8 SA	0432 / 1052 / 1655 / 2311	1.2 / 4.8 / 1.4 / 4.9	23 SU	0339 / 0958 / 1555 / 2208	1.6 / 4.5 / 1.8 / 4.7
9 SU	0531 / 1157 / 1758	1.4 / 4.6 / 1.7	24 M	0426 / 1046 / 1651 / 2300	1.8 / 4.4 / 2.0 / 4.5
10 M	0020 / 0639 / 1304 / 1911	4.7 / 1.6 / 4.6 / 1.7	25 TU	0534 / 1145 / 1808	1.9 / 4.4 / 2.0
11 TU	0129 / 0751 / 1407 / 2023	4.7 / 1.6 / 4.6 / 1.7	26 W	0004 / 0650 / 1255 / 1922	4.5 / 1.8 / 4.4 / 1.9
12 W	0232 / 0856 / 1505 / 2125	4.7 / 1.5 / 4.8 / 1.5	27 TH	0118 / 0758 / 1409 / 2030	4.6 / 1.7 / 4.6 / 1.6
13 TH	0329 / 0952 / 1557 / 2218	4.8 / 1.3 / 4.9 / 1.3	28 F	0235 / 0901 / 1515 / 2132	4.7 / 1.4 / 4.9 / 1.3
14 F	0419 / 1041 / 1642 / 2305	4.9 / 1.1 / 5.1 / 1.1	29 SA	0342 / 1000 / 1612 / 2230	4.9 / 1.1 / 5.1 / 1.0
15 SA	0503 / 1125 / 1721 / 2347	5.0 / 1.0 / 5.2 / 1.0	30 SU	0438 / 1056 / 1704 / 2325	5.1 / 0.9 / 5.4 / 0.7

JULY

Day	Time	m	Day	Time	m
1 M O	0531 / 1149 / 1754	5.3 / 0.6 / 5.5	16 TU	0007 / 0556 / 1222 / 1810	1.1 / 5.0 / 1.1 / 5.2
2 TU	0017 / 0623 / 1241 / 1844	0.5 / 5.4 / 0.5 / 5.7	17 W	0043 / 0634 / 1256 / 1847	1.0 / 5.0 / 1.1 / 5.2
3 W	0108 / 0715 / 1331 / 1934	0.4 / 5.4 / 0.5 / 5.7	18 TH	0116 / 0712 / 1326 / 1924	1.1 / 5.0 / 1.1 / 5.2
4 TH	0157 / 0806 / 1418 / 2022	0.3 / 5.4 / 0.5 / 5.6	19 F	0145 / 0750 / 1355 / 2000	1.1 / 4.9 / 1.2 / 5.1
5 F	0243 / 0854 / 1502 / 2109	0.4 / 5.3 / 0.6 / 5.5	20 SA	0213 / 0825 / 1422 / 2032	1.2 / 4.8 / 1.3 / 5.0
6 SA	0327 / 0941 / 1545 / 2156	0.6 / 5.2 / 0.9 / 5.3	21 SU	0240 / 0857 / 1451 / 2103	1.3 / 4.8 / 1.4 / 4.9
7 SU	0411 / 1030 / 1630 / 2245	0.9 / 4.9 / 1.2 / 5.0	22 M	0309 / 0928 / 1523 / 2137	1.4 / 4.6 / 1.5 / 4.8
8 M	0459 / 1123 / 1721 / 2344	1.3 / 4.7 / 1.6 / 4.7	23 TU	0345 / 1008 / 1606 / 2222	1.6 / 4.5 / 1.7 / 4.7
9 TU	0555 / 1225 / 1823	1.6 / 4.5 / 1.8	24 W	0435 / 1100 / 1708 / 2322	1.7 / 4.5 / 1.9 / 4.5
10 W	0052 / 0704 / 1330 / 1940	4.5 / 1.8 / 4.5 / 1.9	25 TH	0552 / 1207 / 1837	1.9 / 4.4 / 2.0
11 TH	0200 / 0819 / 1432 / 2054	4.4 / 1.8 / 4.5 / 1.8	26 F	0035 / 0721 / 1326 / 1959	4.5 / 1.8 / 4.5 / 1.8
12 F	0301 / 0924 / 1528 / 2154	4.5 / 1.7 / 4.7 / 1.6	27 SA	0200 / 0835 / 1445 / 2109	4.6 / 1.6 / 4.8 / 1.4
13 SA	0354 / 1017 / 1616 / 2243	4.7 / 1.4 / 4.9 / 1.4	28 SU	0319 / 0941 / 1550 / 2213	4.8 / 1.3 / 5.1 / 1.1
14 SU	0439 / 1103 / 1657 / 2327	4.8 / 1.3 / 5.0 / 1.2	29 M	0421 / 1041 / 1646 / 2311	5.1 / 0.9 / 5.4 / 0.7
15 M ●	0519 / 1144 / 1734	4.9 / 1.1 / 5.2	30 TU O	0516 / 1136 / 1738	5.3 / 0.6 / 5.6
			31 W	0004 / 0608 / 1228 / 1829	0.4 / 5.4 / 0.4 / 5.7

AUGUST

Day	Time	m	Day	Time	m
1 TH	0055 / 0700 / 1316 / 1919	0.2 / 5.5 / 0.3 / 5.8	16 F	0053 / 0652 / 1304 / 1906	1.0 / 5.1 / 1.0 / 5.3
2 F	0141 / 0750 / 1401 / 2007	0.1 / 5.5 / 0.3 / 5.8	17 SA	0121 / 0730 / 1332 / 1941	1.0 / 5.1 / 1.0 / 5.2
3 SA	0225 / 0836 / 1443 / 2051	0.2 / 5.4 / 0.4 / 5.6	18 SU	0148 / 0804 / 1359 / 2012	1.0 / 5.0 / 1.1 / 5.1
4 SU	0305 / 0917 / 1522 / 2131	0.5 / 5.3 / 0.7 / 5.3	19 M	0215 / 0833 / 1427 / 2040	1.1 / 4.9 / 1.2 / 5.0
5 M	0344 / 0957 / 1601 / 2210	0.9 / 5.0 / 1.1 / 5.0	20 TU	0243 / 0901 / 1458 / 2112	1.2 / 4.8 / 1.4 / 4.9
6 TU	0424 / 1038 / 1643 / 2251	1.3 / 4.7 / 1.6 / 4.6	21 W	0317 / 0937 / 1537 / 2155	1.4 / 4.7 / 1.6 / 4.7
7 W	0510 / 1130 / 1736 / 2253	1.7 / 4.5 / 2.0 / 4.5	22 TH	0401 / 1028 / 1631 / 2253	1.7 / 4.6 / 1.8 / 4.5
8 TH	0000 / 0609 / 1248 / 1848	4.3 / 2.1 / 4.3 / 2.2	23 F	0505 / 1135 / 1758	1.9 / 4.5 / 2.0
9 F	0127 / 0733 / 1400 / 2021	4.2 / 2.2 / 4.4 / 2.1	24 SA	0009 / 0649 / 1258 / 1936	4.4 / 2.0 / 4.5 / 1.9
10 SA	0235 / 0856 / 1502 / 2131	4.3 / 2.0 / 4.6 / 1.8	25 SU	0140 / 0816 / 1425 / 2055	4.5 / 1.8 / 4.8 / 1.5
11 SU	0331 / 0955 / 1552 / 2222	4.5 / 1.7 / 4.8 / 1.5	26 M	0306 / 0928 / 1535 / 2200	4.8 / 1.4 / 5.1 / 1.1
12 M	0418 / 1041 / 1634 / 2306	4.7 / 1.4 / 5.0 / 1.3	27 TU	0409 / 1029 / 1631 / 2257	5.1 / 0.9 / 5.5 / 0.7
13 TU	0458 / 1122 / 1712 / 2345	4.9 / 1.2 / 5.2 / 1.1	28 W O	0503 / 1122 / 1723 / 2349	5.4 / 0.6 / 5.7 / 0.3
14 W ●	0536 / 1200 / 1750	5.0 / 1.1 / 5.3	29 TH	0553 / 1211 / 1812	5.5 / 0.3 / 5.8
15 TH	0020 / 0613 / 1234 / 1828	1.0 / 5.1 / 1.0 / 5.3	30 F	0036 / 0641 / 1257 / 1859	0.1 / 5.6 / 0.2 / 5.9
			31 SA	0121 / 0727 / 1340 / 1945	0.1 / 5.6 / 0.2 / 5.8

Chart Datum: 3·22 metres below Ordnance Datum (Newlyn)

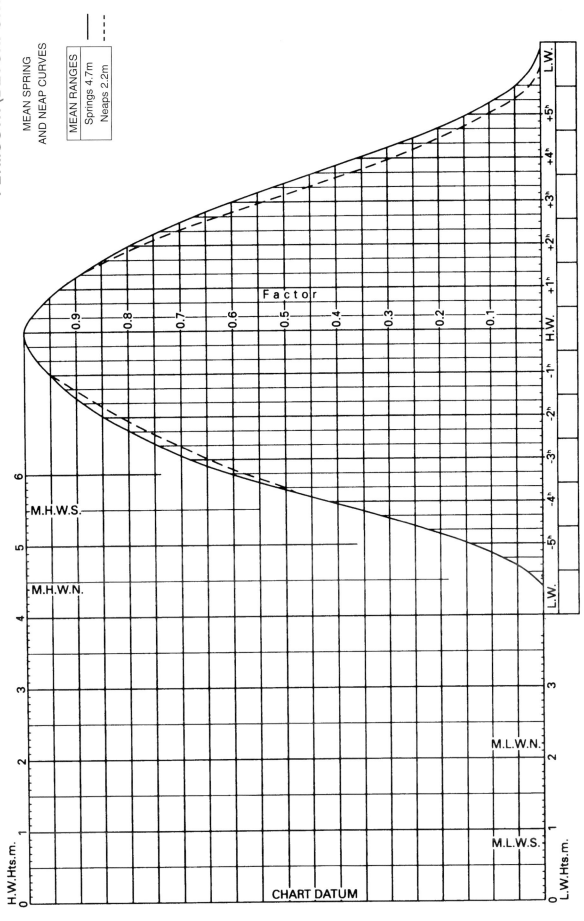

PLYMOUTH (DEVONPORT)

MEAN SPRING
AND NEAP CURVES

MEAN RANGES
Springs 4.7m
Neaps 2.2m

RIVER YEALM

CHARTS
AC *9219*,1900,*1613;* Imray C6, C14; Stanfords 13; OS 201.

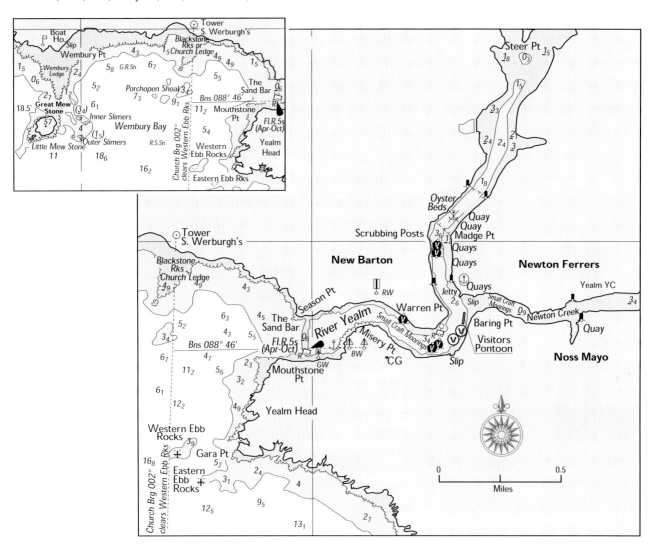

Standard Port PLYMOUTH (←)

Times				Height (metres)			
High Water		Low Water		MHWS	MHWN	MLWN	MLWS
0000	0600	0000	0600	5.5	4.4	2.2	0.8
1200	1800	1200	1800				

Differences RIVER YEALM ENTRANCE
+0006	+0006	+0002	+0002	-0.1	-0.1	-0.1	-0.1

Note: Strong SW winds hold up the ebb and raise levels, as does the river if in spate.

SHELTER
Very good. Ent easy except in strong onshore winds. anchorage in Cellar Bay is open to NW winds. visitors pontoon in The Pool.

NAVIGATION
240°/060° from/to Season Pt, The W & E Ebb rks and the Inner & Outer Slimers are dangerous. lying awash on E and W sides of Wembury Bay. Ldg bns (W ▲, B stripe) in line at 089° clear Mouthstone Ledge, but not the sand bar. The PHM buoy, Fl R 5s (Apr-Oct), marks end of sand bar and must be left to port on entry. When abeam, but not before, bn (G ▲ on W □) on S shore, turn NE toward bn (W □, R stripe) on N shore. From sand bar to Misery Pt, river carries only 1.2m at MLWS. Leave Spit PHM buoy off Warren Pt to port. It is impossible to beat in against an ebb tide. Speed limit 6kn.

LIGHTS AND MARKS
Great Mewstone (57m) is conspic 1.5M to W of river ent. Bns as above. No lights apart from PHM By Fl R 5s at ent.

TELEPHONE (Dial code 01752)
Hr Mr 872533; MRSC (01803) 882704; Customs 0345231110 (H24); Marinecall 0891 500458; Police 701188; Dr 880392.

RADIO TELEPHONE None.

FACILITIES
Yealm Pool M, pontoon £8, L, FW; **Yealm YC**, FW, Bar; **Newton Ferrers** L, Slip, FW, V, Gas, Gaz, R, Bar.

Services: ME, El, Sh, SM. **Bridgend** L, Slip (HW±2¹/₂), FW; **Noss Mayo** L, Slip, FW, V, R, Bar, Nearest fuel 3M at Yealmpton.

ADJACENT ANCHORAGES IN BIGBURY BAY
RIVER ERME, Devon, *AC 1613.* HW0525 on Dover; +0015 and 0.6m on HW Devonport. Temp day anchorage in 3m at mouth of drying river, open to SW. Access near HW, but only in offshore winds and settled, wx. Beware Wells Rk (1.2m) 1M SE of ent. Appr from SW, clear of Edwards Rk. Ent between Battisborough Is and W. Mary's Rk (dries 1.1m) keeping to the W. No facilities.

RIVER AVON, Devon, AC *1613.* Tides as R Erme, above. Enter drying river HW -1, only in offshore winds and settled wx. Appr close E of conspic Burgh Is & Murray's Rks, marked by bn. Narrow chan hugs cliffy NW shore, then turns SE and N off Bantham. A recce at LW or local knowledge would assist. Streams run hard, but able to dry out in good shelter clear of moorings. V, Bar at Bantham. Aveton Gifford accessible by dinghy, 2.5M.

HOPE COVE, AC *1613.* Tides as R Erme, above; ML 2.6m; Duration 0615. Popular day anchorage in centre of cove, but poor holding ground and only safe in offshore winds. Appr with old LB ho brg 110°. and anchor SW of pier hd. Beware rk, drying 2.5m, ¹/₂ca offshore and 3ca E of Bolt Tail. No lts. Facilities: very limited in village, EC Thurs; but good at Kingsbridge (6M bus), or Salcombe, (4M bus).

SALCOMBE

CHARTS
AC *28*, 1634, *1613*; Imray C6, Y48; Stanfords 13; OS 202

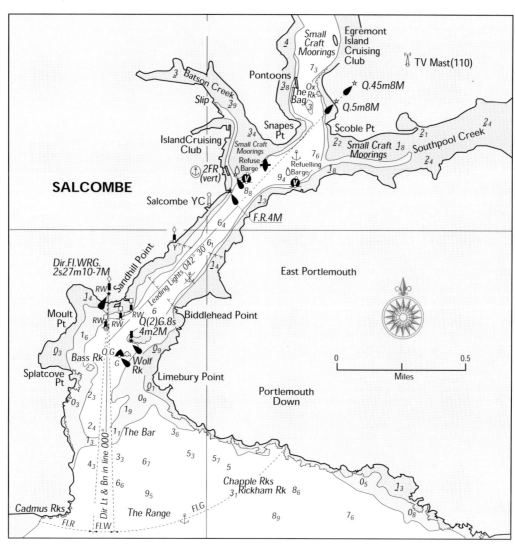

Standard Port PLYMOUTH (←)

Times				Height (metres)			
High Water		Low Water		MHWS	MHWN	MLWN	MLWS
0100	0600	0100	0600	5.5	4.4	2.2	0.8
1300	1800	1300	1800				
Differences SALCOMBE							
0000	+0010	+0005	-0005	-0.2	-0.3	-0.1	-0.1
START POINT							
+0005	+0030	-0005	+0005	-0.2	-0.4	-0.1	-0.1

SHELTER
Perfectly protected hbr but ent exposed to S winds. The estuary is 4M long and has 8 drying creeks off it. Limited anchorage on SE side between ferry and anchoring prohib area. Plenty of deep water visitors moorings. (Hr Mr's launch will contact VHF Ch14, on duty 0600-2100 in season; 0600-2200 in peak season). S'ly winds can cause an uncomfortable swell in the anchorage off the town. Visitors' pontoon and visitors moorings in the Bag are well sheltered. Short stay pontoon (1 hour max, 0700-1900) by Hr Mr's office has 1m. Water taxi via Hr Mr, VHF Ch 12.

NAVIGATION
180°/000° from/to Sandhill Pt lt. The bar (0.7m) can be dangerous at sp ebb tides with strong on-shore winds. Access HW±4½, but at springs this window applies only if swell height does not exceed 1m. The Bar is not as dangerous as rumour may have it, except in the above conditions; if in doubt, call Hr Mr Ch 14 before approaching. Rickham Rk, E of the Bar, has 3.lm depth. Speed limit 8kn; radar checks in force.

Note: The site of a Historic Wreck is at Moor Sand, 1M WNW of Prawle Pt.

LIGHTS AND MARKS
Outer ldg marks: Sandhill Pt bn on with Poundstone bn 000°. Sandhill Pt Dir lt 000°, Fl WRG 2s 27m l0/7M; R and W♦ on W mast: vis R002°-182°, G182°-357°, W357°-002°. Beware unmarked Bass Rk (dries 0.8m) close W of ldg line and Wolf Rk, marked by SHM By QG, close E of ldg line. After passing Wolf Rk, pick up Inner ldg lts, Q Fl 042°, leaving Blackstone Rk Q (2) G 8s 4m 2M to stbd.

RADIO TELEPHONE
VHF Ch 14 call *Salcombe Hbr or Launch* (Mon-Thurs 0900-1645, Fri 0900-1615); 14 May-14 Sept Sat/Sun 0900-1615). Call *Water taxi* Ch 12. Call: *ICC Base* (clubhouse) and *Egremont* (ICC floating HQ) Ch M. *Fuel Barge* Ch 06.

TELEPHONE (Dial code 01548)
Hr Mr 843791, MRSC (01803) 882704; Customs 0345 231110 (H24); Marinecall 0891 500458; Police; 842107; Dr 842284.

FACILITIES
Harbour (300+150 visitors) £10 for visitors berths. M, Slip, P, D, L, ME, El, C (15 ton), Sh, CH, SM, Water Taxi; FW at visitors' pontoon by Hr Mr's Office or from water boat; if needed, fly a bucket in the rigging. Public slipway at Batson Creek.

Salcombe YC, L, R, Bar;

Island Cruising Club, Bar.

Services: Slip, M, P, D, FW, ME, CH, El, Sh, ACA, SM;

Fuel Barge (0836) 775644 or (01752) 223434, D, P.

Town EC Thurs; all facilities.

BRIXHAM

CHARTS
AC *26, 1613, 1634,* 3315; Imray C5, Y43; Stanfords 12; OS 202

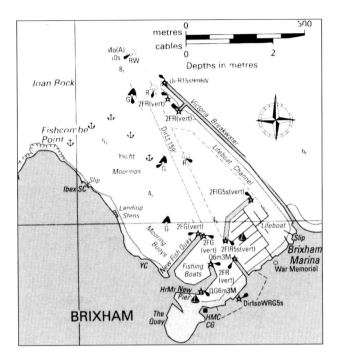

Standard Port PLYMOUTH (←)

Times				Height (metres)			
High Water		Low Water		MHWS	MHWN	MLWN	MLWS
0100	0600	0100	0600	5.5	4.4	2.2	0.8
1300	1800	1300	1800				
Differences BRIXHAM							
+0025	+0045	+0010	0000	-0.6	-0.7	-0.2	-0.1

Note: There is often a stand of about 1 hour at HW

SHELTER
Very good in marina; also at YC pontoon in SW corner of hbr, but outer hbr is dangerous in NW winds. visitors buoys (W) to E of main fairway. Inner hbr dries. To W of hbr are anchorages in Fishcombe Cove and Elberry Cove (beware water skiers).

NAVIGATION
050°/230° from/to Victoria bkwtr It. No dangers; easy access. Note: Around Torbay are controlled areas, close inshore and marked by Y SPM buoys, mainly for swimmers; boats may enter with caution, speed limit 5kn.

LIGHTS AND MARKS
Berry Hd It, Fl (2)15s 58m 15M, is 1.2M ESE of ent. Bkwtr hd Oc R 15s 9m 6M, W tr. 3 R● or 3 ® Its (vert) at ent = hbr closed. At SE end of hbr a Dir It iso WRG 5s 4m 6M, vis G145°-157°, W157°-161°, R161°-173° leads 159° into the fairway, marked by two pairs of lateral It buoys.

RADIO TELEPHONE
Marina: Ch 80. YC and Water Taxi: *Shuttle* Ch M. Hr Mr Ch 14 16 (May-Sept 0800-1800LT; Oct-Apr 0900- 1700, Mon-Fri). Brixham CG: Ch 16 10 67 73.

TELEPHONE (Dial code 01803)
Marina 882929; Hr Mr 853321; Pilot 882214; MRSC 882704; Customs 0345 231110 (H24); Marinecall 0891 500458; Police 882231; Dr 882731.

FACILITIES
Marina (480 inc visitors) £13.75, Access H24, AC, FW, D (0900-2000, Apr-Sep inc), R, Bar, Hbr Office (New Fish Quay) Slip, M, L, FW, C (2 ton), AB, D; Brixham YC pontoon, M, L, Slip, FW, R, Bar;
Services: CH, ACA. ME, (H24), P (cans), El, Town EC Wed; R, Bar.

TORQUAY

CHARTS
AC 26, 1613, 3315; Imray C5, Y43; Stanfords 12; OS 202

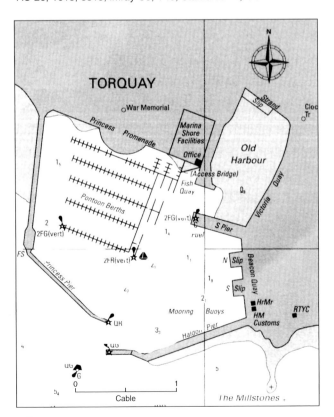

Standard Port PLYMOUTH (←)

Times				Height (metres)			
High Water		Low Water		MHWS	MHWN	MLWN	MLWS
0100	0600	0100	0600	5.5	4.4	2.2	0.8
1300	1800	1300	1800				
Differences TORQUAY							
+0025	+0045	+0010	0000	-0.6	-0.7	-0.2	-0.1

Note: There is often a stand of about 1 hour at HW

SHELTER
Good, but some swell in hbr with strong SE winds, which may make the narrow ent difficult due to backwash. No anchoring within hbr. NW of Hope's Nose there are anchorages at Hope Cove, Anstey's Cove and Babbacombe Bay, sheltered in W'lies.

NAVIGATION
165°/345° from/to Haldon pier It. Access at all tides. Inner (Old) hbr dries completely. Speed limit 5kn. 3 R ● or 3 R Its = hbr closed.

LIGHTS AND MARKS
No ldg marks/Its. Princess Pier head QR 9m 6M. Haldon pier hd QG 9m 6M. S pier hd 2FG (vert) 5M. All Its may be difficult to discern against town Its.

RADIO TELEPHONE
Port VHF Ch 14 16 (May-Sept 0800-1800LT; Oct-Apr 0900-1700, Mon-Fri). Marina Ch 80 (H24), M. *Torquay Fuel* Ch M.

TELEPHONE (Dial code 01803)
Hr Mr 292429; MRSC 882704; Police 0990 777444; Marinecall 0891 500458; Dr 212429.

FACILITIES
Marina (440+60 visitors) £17.30, FW, ME, Gas, Gaz, AC, SM, El, Sh, CH, V, R, Bar, ACA. **S Pier** FW, C (6 ton), P & D: Torquay Fuel 294509/mobile 0385 226839 & VHF Ch M Apr-Sept, 0830-1900 Mon-Sat, 1000-1900 Sun); **Haldon Pier** FW, AB; **Princess Pier** L; **Royal Torbay YC** 292006, R, Bar. Town V, R, Bar.

BRAYE (Alderney)

CHARTS
AC *2845, 60, 3653, 2669;* SHOM 6934, 7158; ECM 1014;
Imray C33A; Stanfords 7,16

Standard Port ST HELIER (→)

Times				Height (metres)			
High Water		Low Water		MHWS	MHWN	MLWN	MLWS
0300	0900	0200	0900	11.0	8.1	4.0	1.4
1500	2100	1400	2100				
Differences BRAYE							
+0050	+0040	+0025	+0105	-4.8	-3.4	-1.5	-0.5

SHELTER
Good in Braye Hbr, except in strong N/NE winds. 80 Y visitors buoys lie parallel to the Admiralty bkwtr and near Fort Albert. Orange buoys are for locals. No landing on Admiralty bkwtr; at its NE end beware submerged extension. Anchorage in hbr is good on sand, but only fair on rock or weed patches; keep clear of the fairway and jetty due to steamer traffic. Hbr speed limit 4kn. Access to inner hbr HW±2 for D, FW.

NAVIGATION
035°/215° from/to front ldg lt 215°. The main hazards are strong tidal streams and the many rocks encircling Alderney. The safest appr is from the NE. Take the Swinge and the Race at/near slack water to avoid the dangerous overfalls in certain wind and tide conditions. In the Swinge calmest area is often near Corbet Rk, bn 'C'. At mid-flood (NE-going) a strong eddy flows SW past the hbr ent. On the S side of the island during the ebb, a strong NE-going eddy runs close inshore of Coque Lihou. Give Brinchetais Ledge (E end) a wide berth to avoid heavy overfalls. An Historic Wreck is 5ca N of Quenard Pt lt ho.

LIGHTS AND MARKS
From NW, N side of Ft Albert and end of Admiralty bkwtr 115° clear the Nannels. Iso WR 4s at Chateau á l'Etoc Pt, E of the hbr, vis R071°-111°, W111°-151°, in line 111° with Quenard Pt lt ho, Fl (4)l5s, clears sunken ruins of bkwtr. Ldg lts, both Q vis 210°-220°, lead 215° into hbr; front 8m 17M; rear 17m 18M. The Admty bkwtr hd has a lt, L Fl l0s 7m 5M. By day, St Anne's church spire on with W bn at Douglas Quay leads 210° to fairway which is marked by a QR and QG buoy and an inner pair of Q (2) R 5s and Q (2) G 5s buoys. End of steamer quay has 2 FR (vert) lts.

RADIO TELEPHONE
Call: *Alderney Radio* VHF Ch **74** 16 (12) (Apr to Sept, 0800 - 1800, daily; Oct 0800-1700 daily; Nov to Mar, 0800-1700, Mon-Fri: all LT). Note: In fog/limited vis radar assistance to small craft is available from Hr Mr during above hrs. Outside these hrs call St Peter Port. For the Casquets TSS see Cherbourg. Mainbrayce Marine Ch 80 M (Apr-mid Sept: 0800-2000LT). Water taxi call *Mainbrayce* Ch M, 0800-2359.

TELEPHONE (*Dial code 01481*)
Hr Mr 822620; Marinecail 0891 500 432; Police 822731;
Dr 822077.

FACILITIES
Hbr buoys (£10 for <12m LOA, £12 for >12m); **Jetty**, FW, C; **Sapper Slip**, FW; **Alderney SC** 822758, Bar; **Services**: Slip, FW, ME, El, Gas, SM, Sh, CH, ACA, P (cans), D (Mainbrayce, inner hbr HW±2). **Town** EC Wed; V, R, Bar, Ferry: via Guernsey - Poole.

ANCHORAGES AROUND ALDERNEY
There are several anchorages, all picturesque but only safe in off-shore winds. None provide any facilities; clockwise from BRAYE:

SAYE BAY, Small sandy bay adjacent to Braye.
CORBLET BAY, A clear bay in NE corner of the island.
LONGY BAY, Wide sandy bay with good holding in sand. Anchor between Essex Castle and Raz Is to await fair tide in the Race.
LA TCHUE, Good holding in small bay surrounded by cliffs.
TELEGRAPH BAY, Pleasant sandy bay on SW tip of the island.
HANNAINE BAY, A good place to wait for the flood tide.
PLATTE SALINE BAY, Good shelter from E winds.
BURHOU, anchor in bay in SW of the islands, below half tide.

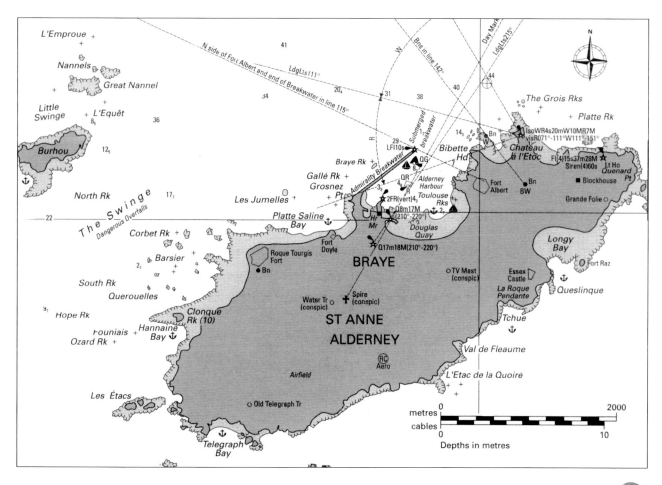

CHANNEL ISLANDS - ST. HELIER

TIMES AND HEIGHTS OF HIGH AND LOW WATERS

MAY

Day		Time	m	Time	m	Time	m	Time	m
1	W	0448	9.6	1126	2.1	1715	10.0	2348	1.9
2	TH	0532	10.3	1212	1.6	1756	10.6		
3	F O	0034	1.4	0613	10.8	1256	1.2	1834	11.0
4	SA	0117	1.0	0653	11.1	1337	1.0	1913	11.3
5	SU	0159	0.9	0733	11.2	1417	1.0	1952	11.3
6	M	0239	0.9	0814	11.0	1456	1.2	2033	11.0
7	TU	0320	1.2	0857	10.6	1537	1.6	2117	10.5
8	W	0404	1.6	0945	10.0	1624	2.2	2207	9.9
9	TH	0456	2.2	1041	9.4	1720	2.8	2307	9.3
10	F	0559	2.6	1148	8.9	1830	3.1		
11	SA	0019	8.9	0712	2.8	1305	8.7	1947	3.2
12	SU	0138	8.8	0826	2.8	1423	8.8	2100	2.9
13	M	0253	9.1	0933	2.5	1530	9.2	2205	2.5
14	TU	0356	9.5	1034	2.1	1625	9.7	2303	2.1
15	W	0450	9.9	1128	1.8	1714	10.2	2355	1.7
16	TH	0538	10.3	1218	1.5	1757	10.5		
17	F ●	0043	1.5	0621	10.6	1303	1.4	1837	10.8
18	SA	0126	1.3	0701	10.6	1342	1.4	1914	10.8
19	SU	0202	1.4	0738	10.5	1416	1.6	1948	10.7
20	M	0234	1.6	0812	10.2	1445	1.9	2019	10.3
21	TU	0303	2.0	0843	9.8	1513	2.3	2049	9.9
22	W	0330	2.4	0914	9.3	1540	2.8	2120	9.4
23	TH	0358	2.9	0946	8.8	1611	3.2	2153	8.9
24	F	0432	3.3	1025	8.4	1651	3.6	2235	8.4
25	SA	0518	3.6	1115	8.0	1745	3.9	2332	8.1
26	SU	0621	3.8	1223	7.9	1858	4.0		
27	M	0044	8.0	0735	3.8	1339	8.0	2012	3.8
28	TU	0159	8.3	0835	3.5	1448	8.5	2118	3.4
29	W	0307	8.7	0949	3.0	1548	9.1	2218	2.8
30	TH	0407	9.3	1047	2.4	1640	9.8	2314	2.2
31	F	0500	10.0	1140	1.9	1728	10.4		

JUNE

Day		Time	m	Time	m	Time	m	Time	m
1	SA O	0006	1.6	0549	10.5	1231	1.4	1813	11.0
2	SU	0056	1.1	0636	11.0	1318	1.1	1857	11.3
3	M	0144	0.8	0721	11.2	1404	1.0	1941	11.5
4	TU	0230	0.8	0807	11.2	1449	1.1	2026	11.3
5	W	0316	0.9	0853	10.9	1535	1.4	2112	11.0
6	TH	0403	1.3	0942	10.5	1623	1.9	2202	10.5
7	F	0453	1.8	1034	9.9	1715	2.4	2256	9.9
8	SA	0548	2.3	1131	9.4	1815	2.8	2357	9.4
9	SU	0650	2.7	1235	9.0	1920	3.1		
10	M	0104	9.0	0755	2.9	1346	8.9	2028	3.2
11	TU	0216	8.9	0900	2.9	1454	9.0	2133	3.1
12	W	0323	9.0	1002	2.8	1554	9.2	2234	2.8
13	TH	0423	9.3	1100	2.6	1647	9.6	2329	2.5
14	F	0514	9.6	1151	2.4	1733	10.0		
15	SA	0018	2.2	0559	9.9	1237	2.1	1814	10.3
16	SU ●	0101	2.0	0640	10.1	1317	2.0	1852	10.4
17	M	0139	1.9	0718	10.2	1352	2.0	1928	10.5
18	TU	0213	1.9	0753	10.1	1425	2.1	2001	10.3
19	W	0245	2.1	0826	9.9	1456	2.3	2033	10.0
20	TH	0315	2.3	0858	9.6	1525	2.5	2104	9.7
21	F	0344	2.6	0929	9.2	1555	2.8	2135	9.3
22	SA	0414	2.9	1002	8.9	1629	3.2	2210	9.0
23	SU	0451	3.1	1041	8.6	1711	3.4	2255	8.7
24	M	0537	3.4	1131	8.4	1806	3.7	2351	8.5
25	TU	0636	3.5	1234	8.3	1915	3.7		
26	W	0100	8.4	0748	3.5	1348	8.4	2030	3.5
27	TH	0215	8.6	0903	3.3	1503	8.8	2140	3.1
28	F	0328	9.0	1012	2.8	1608	9.5	2245	2.5
29	SA	0433	9.6	1114	2.2	1706	10.2	2344	1.8
30	SU	0531	10.3	1211	1.6	1758	10.8		

JULY

Day		Time	m	Time	m	Time	m	Time	m
1	M O	0039	1.2	0623	10.8	1305	1.2	1846	11.4
2	TU	0132	0.8	0713	11.3	1355	0.9	1933	11.7
3	W	0221	0.6	0800	11.4	1442	0.8	2019	11.7
4	TH	0309	0.6	0845	11.3	1528	1.0	2104	11.5
5	F	0354	0.9	0931	11.0	1613	1.4	2149	11.0
6	SA	0439	1.4	1017	10.5	1659	2.0	2236	10.3
7	SU	0526	2.0	1105	9.8	1747	2.6	2327	9.6
8	M	0616	2.7	1158	9.2	1842	3.2		
9	TU	0025	9.0	0713	3.2	1302	8.7	1945	3.6
10	W	0134	8.6	0819	3.5	1413	8.6	2056	3.7
11	TH	0248	8.5	0927	3.6	1522	8.7	2204	3.5
12	F	0355	8.7	1030	3.3	1621	9.1	2303	3.2
13	SA	0451	9.1	1124	3.0	1710	9.5	2352	2.8
14	SU	0538	9.5	1210	2.6	1753	10.0		
15	M ●	0036	2.4	0619	9.9	1251	2.3	1831	10.3
16	TU	0115	2.1	0657	10.1	1329	2.1	1907	10.5
17	W	0151	2.0	0732	10.2	1405	2.0	1942	10.5
18	TH	0226	1.9	0806	10.1	1438	2.0	2014	10.3
19	F	0258	2.0	0838	9.9	1509	2.2	2045	10.1
20	SA	0326	2.2	0907	9.7	1537	2.4	2114	9.8
21	SU	0354	2.5	0937	9.4	1607	2.7	2145	9.5
22	M	0425	2.7	1010	9.1	1643	3.0	2224	9.2
23	TU	0503	3.0	1052	8.8	1727	3.3	2312	8.9
24	W	0553	3.3	1147	8.6	1826	3.6		
25	TH	0015	8.6	0658	3.5	1300	8.4	1945	3.6
26	F	0134	8.5	0822	3.5	1426	8.6	2109	3.3
27	SA	0259	8.7	0944	3.1	1544	9.1	2222	2.7
28	SU	0415	9.3	1054	2.5	1650	9.9	2327	2.0
29	M	0519	10.0	1156	1.8	1746	10.7		
30	TU O	0025	1.3	0613	10.8	1252	1.1	1835	11.4
31	W	0119	0.7	0701	11.4	1343	0.6	1922	11.9

AUGUST

Day		Time	m	Time	m	Time	m	Time	m
1	TH	0209	0.3	0747	11.7	1430	0.4	2005	12.0
2	F	0254	0.3	0830	11.7	1513	0.6	2047	11.8
3	SA	0336	0.5	0911	11.4	1554	1.0	2128	11.3
4	SU	0416	1.1	0951	10.8	1633	1.7	2209	10.6
5	M	0454	1.9	1032	10.0	1711	2.5	2252	9.7
6	TU	0534	2.8	1116	9.2	1755	3.3	2342	8.9
7	W	0623	3.6	1212	8.5	1852	4.0		
8	TH	0048	8.2	0727	4.1	1328	8.1	2009	4.3
9	F	0212	8.0	0847	4.2	1449	8.2	2134	4.1
10	SA	0329	8.3	1000	3.9	1555	8.7	2238	3.6
11	SU	0428	8.8	1056	3.3	1647	9.2	2326	3.0
12	M	0514	9.3	1143	2.8	1729	9.8		
13	TU	0009	2.5	0554	9.8	1225	2.3	1808	10.3
14	W ●	0049	2.1	0632	10.2	1304	2.0	1844	10.6
15	TH	0127	1.8	0707	10.4	1341	1.8	1919	10.7
16	F	0202	1.7	0741	10.4	1416	1.7	1951	10.6
17	SA	0235	1.7	0813	10.3	1447	1.8	2021	10.4
18	SU	0303	1.9	0841	10.1	1516	2.0	2049	10.2
19	M	0330	2.1	0909	9.8	1544	2.3	2119	9.9
20	TU	0359	2.4	0940	9.5	1616	2.6	2155	9.5
21	W	0434	2.8	1019	9.1	1656	3.0	2240	9.0
22	TH	0519	3.2	1111	8.7	1751	3.4	2343	8.5
23	F	0622	3.6	1225	8.3	1911	3.7		
24	SA	0107	8.2	0752	3.7	1402	8.4	2045	3.5
25	SU	0242	8.4	0924	3.3	1528	8.9	2205	2.8
26	M	0402	9.1	1038	2.6	1635	9.8	2312	2.0
27	TU	0505	10.0	1140	1.8	1731	10.7		
28	W O	0009	1.2	0557	10.8	1236	1.0	1819	11.5
29	TH	0102	0.5	0644	11.4	1326	0.5	1904	12.0
30	F	0149	0.2	0727	11.8	1411	0.3	1946	12.2
31	SA	0232	0.1	0808	11.8	1452	0.4	2025	11.9

Chart Datum: 5·88 metres below Ordnance Datum (Local)

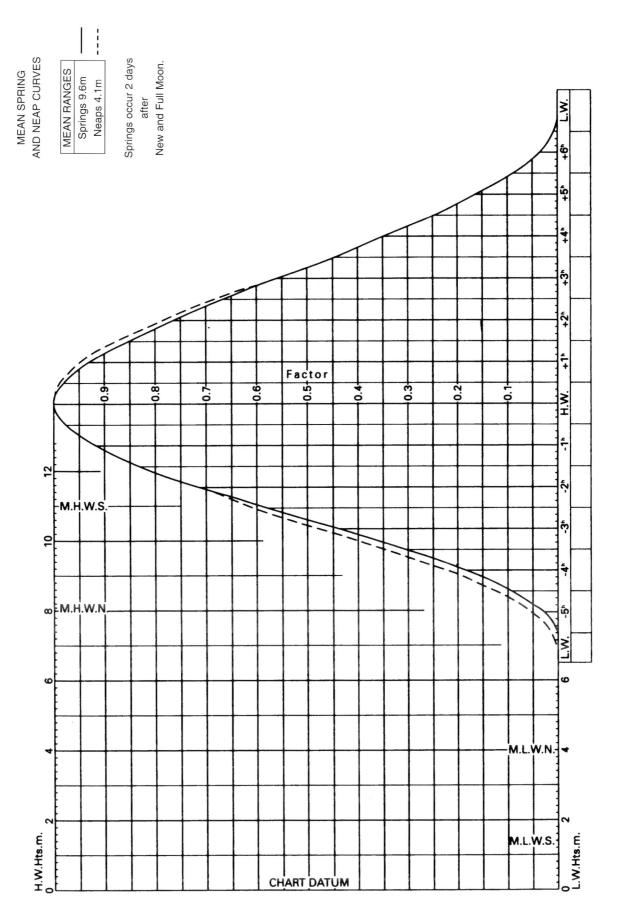

ST. HELIER

MEAN SPRING
AND NEAP CURVES

MEAN RANGES
Springs 9.6m
Neaps 4.1m

Springs occur 2 days
after
New and Full Moon.

OMONVILLE-LA-ROGUE Manche

CHARTS
AC *1106, 2669;* SHOM 5636, 6737, 7158; ECM 528, 1014; Imray C33A; Stanfords 7, 16

TIDES
-0330 Dover; ML 3.6; Duration 0545; Zone -0100

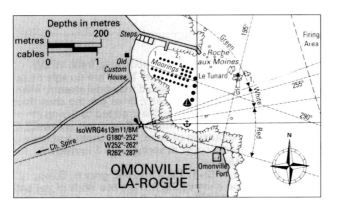

Map: OMONVILLE-LA-ROGUE

Standard Port CHERBOURG (←)

Times				Height (metres)			
High Water		Low Water		MHWS	MHWN	MLWN	MLWS
0300	1000	0400	1000	6.4	5.0	2.5	1.1
1500	2200	1600	2200				
Differences OMONVILLE							
-0025	-0030	-0022	-0022	-0.3	-0.2	-0.2	-0.1
GOURY							
-0100	-0040	-0105	-0120	+1.7	+1.6	+1.0	+0.3

SHELTER
Good, except in strong winds from N to SE. There are 4 W conical visitors bouys or anchor S of bkwtr; beware rks off outer end.

NAVIGATION
075°/255° from/to Omonville lt, 1.0M. Ent is 100m wide, between rks extending N from Omonville Fort, and running ESE from bkwtr marked by Le Tunard, G bn tr. From W or N, keep clear of Basse Bréfort (depth 1m, marked by NCM buoy, VQ) 0.6M N of Pte de Jardeheu. Appr on 195° transit, passing 100m E of Le Tunard and into W sector of lt before turning stbd 290° for old Custom Ho and moorings. From E, appr on 255° transit in W sector of lt, until S of Le Tunard.

To ENE of port is a military firing area; when active, a R flag is flown from the bkwtr head.

LIGHTS AND MARKS
Omonville lt, Iso WRG 4s 13m 11/8M, on W framework tr with R top, vis G180°-252°, W252°-262°, R262°-287°. Lt in transit 255° with church steeple, 650m beyond, leads S of Le Tunard. From N, Le Tunard leads 195° in transit with fort. Street lts adequately illuminate the hbr area.

RADIO TELEPHONE
None. For Casquets TSS see Cherbourg

TELEPHONE (Prefix nos with zone code 02)
Aff Mar Cherbourg 33.53.21.76; Customs) Cherbourg 33.53.05.60;

CROSS 33.52.72.13; 33.52.7 1.33; Météo 33.22.91.77; Auto 08.36.68.08.50; Police 33.52.72.02; Dr 33.53.08.69; Brit Consul 01.33.44.20.13.

FACILITIES
Jetty M, L, FW, AB, V, R, Bar. **Village** V, Gaz, R, Bar, nearest fuel (cans) at Beaumont-Hague 5km, (bus to Cherbourg), Ferry: See Cherbourg.

DIÉLETTE Manche

CHARTS
AC 3653; SHOM 7133,7158; ECM 528, 1014; Imray C33A; Stanfords 16

TIDES
HW -0430 on Dover (UT); ML 5.2m

Standard Port ST-MALO (→)

Times				Height (metres)			
High Water		Low Water		MHWS	MHWN	MLWN	MLWS
0100	0800	0300	0800	12.2	9.2	4.3	1.6
1300	2000	1500	2000				
Differences FLAMANVILLE							
+0050	+0050	+0025	+0045	-2.7	-1.8	-1.1	-0.5

SHELTER
Good in marina, but do not attempt entry in strong W'lies. Ent dredged to CD, NE part of outer hbr to 2m; access H24 for 1.5m draft if coeff <80. W side of outer hbr dries approx 5m (local moorings). Marina (1.5-2.5m) in SE corner is entered over a sill 4.0m above CD; access about HW±3 for 1.5m draft, waiting pontoon outside.

NAVIGATION
320°/140° from/to W bkwtr lt, 0.40M. Appr is exposed to W'ly winds/swell. Caution: rky reef dries close NE of appr; cross tides at hbr ent. Prohib area from hbr to C de Flamanville extends 5ca offshore.

LIGHTS AND MARKS
Power stn chys (72m) are conspic 1.2M to SW. Dir lt 140°, Iso WRG 4s 12m 10/7M, W tr/G top at hd of West bkwtr, vis G070°-135°, W135°-145° (10°), R145°-180°; on same tr is a lower lt, Fl G 4s 6m 2M. N bkwtr hd, Fl R 4s 8m 5M, W mast/R top. Spur, close SE at ent to new basin, is Fl (2) R 6s 6m 1M.

RADIO TELEPHONE
VHF Ch 09, 0830-2000LT.

FACILITIES
Marina (410) FF124, AC, FW, Fuel, Slip, C (10 ton); **Village**, V, Bar, R. Also facilities at Flamanville (1.3M). Ferry to CI.

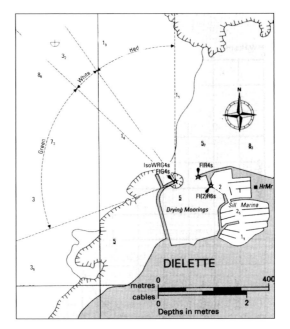

Map: DIELETTE

MINOR HARBOUR CLOSE SOUTH OF CAP DE LA HAGUE
GOURY, Manche, AC *1706, 3653;* SHOM 7133 (essential large scale chart), 5636, 7158. HW -0410 on Dover (UT); ML 5.1m. For visitors, appr at slack water nps with no swell and good vis; a fair wx hbr only, dries to flat sand/mud. Cap de la Hague lt, Fl 5s, is 0.5M NW of hbr; La Foraine WCM buoy is 1.1M to the W. Ldg lts: Front QR 4m 7M, on bkwtr hd; rear (110m from front), Q 10m 12M, intens 057°-075°, lead 065° between Charlin to S and Les Grois to N. By day, W patch with R ■ at end of bkwtr on with W pylon of rear ldg lt, 065°. anchor W of the 2 LB slips in 1.7m or dry out on the NE side of the bkwtr. Facilities: R, Bar at Auderville (0.5M).

CARTERET Manche

CHARTS
AC *3655,2669;* SHOM 7133, 7157, 7158; ECM 1014; Imray C33A; Stanfords 16

TIDES
-0440 Dover; ML 5.9; Duration 0545; Zone -0100

Standard Port ST-MALO (→)

Times				Height (metres)			
High Water		Low Water		MHWS	MHWN	MLWN	MLWS
0100	0800	0300	0800	12.2	9.2	4.3	1.6
1300	2000	1500	2000				
Differences CARTERET							
+0035	+0025	+0020	+0035	-1.6	-1.1	-0.6	-0.3

SHELTER
Good in non-tidal marina (sill is 4m above CD; lifting gate retains 2.3m within); access HW-2½ to +3 for 1.5m draft. Visitors berths on far side of the most E'ly pontoon (F). If too late on the tide for the marina, possible waiting berths on W Jetty (clear of ferry) where a 1.5m draft boat can stay afloat for 6 hrs np, 9hrs sp. The tiny Pont des Américains and drying basin, close W of marina, have up to 5m at HW.

NAVIGATION
189°/009° from/ to W Jetty lt, 1M. From N/NW, keep well offshore on appr to avoid rks 1M N of Cap de Carteret extending about 1M from coast. From W, about 4M off shore, beware Trois Grune Rks (dry 1.6m) marked by WCM buoy,Q (9) 15s.

Appr dries ½M offshore and is exposed to fresh W/SW winds which can make ent rough. There are no safe anchorages off shore. Best appr at HW-2 to avoid max tidal stream, 4½kn sp. Bar, at right angles to W Jetty, dries 4m; the chan dries progressively to firm sand, and is dredged to drying hts of 4m and 4.5m just W of the marina. Best water is toward the W quays and outside of bend. The E bkwtr and head of W bkwtr both partly cover at springs. No anchoring in river.

LIGHTS AND MARKS
Cap de Carteret, Fl (2+1) 15s 81m 26M, grey tr, G top, Horn (3) 60s, and conspic Sig Stn are 8ca WxN of the ent. W Jetty, Oc R 4s 6m 8M, W col, R top; E bkwtr, Fl G 2.5s, W mast G top. These lts in transit lead about 009° to ent. The bend in the chan is marked by a PHM and SHM bn, respectively Fl (2) R 6s & Fl (2) G 6s. Marina sill is marked by a PHM and SHM lt bn, respectively Fl (3) R 12s & Fl (3) G 12s, plus Y poles.

RADIO TELEPHONE
VHF Ch 16 64. Marina Ch 09.

TELEPHONE (Prefix nos with zone code 02)
Hr mr 33.44.00.13; CROSS 33.52.72.13; n 33.04.90.08; Météo 33.22.91.77; Auto 08.36.68.08.50; Police 33.53.80.17; n (Valognes) 33.40.14.39; Brit Consul 01.33.44.20.13.

FACILITIES
Port de Plaisance "Le Port des Iles" 33.04.70.84, (260 + 60 visitors), FF109, AC, FW, CH, Fuel;

West Jetty AB free for 6 hrs, then at 50% of marina rate, Slip, FW, R, Bar;

Cerde Nautique de Barneville-Carteret 33.53.88.29, Slip, M, Bar.

Town ME, P & D (cans), V, Gaz, R, Bar. Ferry: Cherbourg, Jersey.

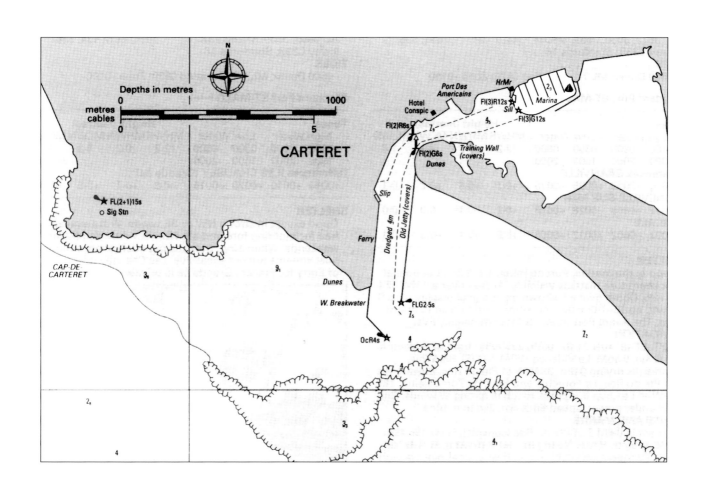

PORTBAIL Manche

CHARTS
AC *3655, 2669;* SHOM 7133, 7157; ECM 1014; Imray C33A; Stanfords 16

TIDES
HW -0440 on Dover (UT); ML 6.3m; Duration 0545

Standard Port ST-MALO (→)

Times				Height (metres)			
High Water		Low Water		MHWS	MHWN	MLWN	MLWS
0100	0800	0300	0800	12.2	9.2	4.3	1.6
1300	2000	1500	2000				
Differences PORTBAIL							
+0035	+0030	+0030	+0035	-0.8	-0.5	-0.3	-0.1
ST GERMAIN-SUR-AY							
+0030	+0030	+0040	+0040	-0.7	-0.4	-0.1	0.0
LE SÉNÉQUET							
+0020	+0020	+0028	+0028	-0.3	-0.2	0.0	0.0

SHELTER
Good. Hbr dries 7.0m, but access HW±1/2 at np, HW±2 1/2 at sp for 1m draft. Drying basin to E of jetty: visitors berth on pontoon parallel with NW side of basin or moor on first line of buoys parallel to jetty. Portbail is 4M SE of Carteret.

NAVIGATION
222°/042° from/to chan buoys, 1.4M. Beware very strong tide over bar. Ldg line crosses sand banks (drying about 8ca offshore) to a pair of unlit PHM/SHM buoys. Thence via chan dredged 5.2m; on port side a training wall (covers at HW) is marked by R spar bns, the first Q (2) R 5s.

LIGHTS AND MARKS
A Water Tr (43m) is conspic 6ca NNW of ent. Ldg Its 042°: Front (La Caillourie) QW 14m 10M, W pylon, R top; rear, 870m from front, Oc 4s 20m 10M (church spire). Training wall hd, Q (2) R 5s 5m 2M.

RADIO TELEPHONE
VHF Ch 09.

TELEPHONE (Prefix nos with zone code 02) Hr Mr 33.04.83.48 (15 Jun-31 Aug).

FACILITIES
Quay FF50, FW, D, P, AC, C (5 ton); Cerde Nautique de Portbail-Denneville 33.04.86.15, Bar, R; YC de Portbail 33.04.83.48, AB, C, Slip; Services: Sh, ME, El. Town (1/2M by causeway) Bar R, V.

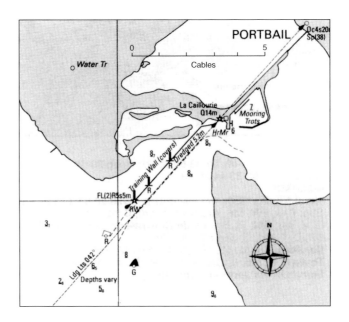

GRANVILLE Manche

CHARTS
AC 3672, *3656, 3659;* SHOM 7341, 7156; ECM 534, 535; Imray C33B; Stanfords 16

TIDES
-0510 Dover; ML 7.1; Duration 0525; Zone-0100

Standard Port ST-MALO (→)

Times				Height (metres)			
High Water		Low Water		MHWS	MHWN	MLWN	MLWS
0100	0800	0300	0800	12.2	9.2	4.3	1.6
1300	2000	1500	2000				
Differences GRANVILLE							
+0019	+0010	+0025	+0015	+0.7	+0.6	+0.2	-0.1
REGNEVILLE-SUR-MER							
+0018	+0018	+0028	+0028	-0.2	-0.1	0.0	0.0

SHELTER
Good in the marina, Port de Herel, 1.5-2.5m. Caution: at ent sharp turn restricts visibility. Access over sill HW -2 1/2 to +3 1/2. Depth over sill shown on lit digital display atop S bkwtr: eg 76=7.6m; 00 = no entry; hard to read in bright sun. The Avant Port (dries) is for commercial/ FVs.

NAVIGATION
235°/055° from/to S bkwtr It (Fl R 4s), 0.95M. Le Videcoq WCM, VQ (9) 10s Whis, marks rks drying 0.8m, 3 1/4 M W of Pte du Roc. Beware rks off Pte du Roc, La Fourchie and Banc de Tombelaine, 1M SSW of Le Loup It. Appr is rough in strong W winds. Ent/ exit under power; speed limit 4kn, 2kn in marina.

LIGHTS AND MARKS
Hbr ent is 0.6M E of Pte du Roc (conspic), Fl (4)15s 49m 23M, grey tr, R top. No ldg Its, but S bkwtr It, Fl R 4s, on with TV mast leads 055° to ent. Best appr at night is with Le Loup bearing 085° to avoid pot markers off Pte du Roc; hbr Its are hard to see against town Its. Turn port at bkwtr to cross the sill between RIG piles, Oc RG 4s. Sill of bathing pool to stbd is marked by 5 R piles, lit Fl Bu 4s.

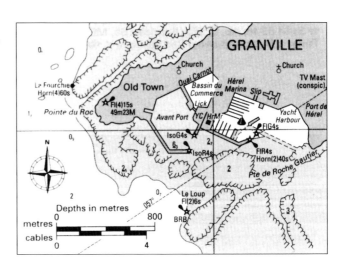

RADIO TELEPHONE
Port VHF Ch 12 16 (HW±1 1/2). Marina Ch 09, H24 in season.

TELEPHONE (Prefix nos with zone code 02)
Hr Mr (Hérel) 33.50.20.06; Hr Mr (Port) 33.50.17.75; Aff Mar 33.50.00.59; CROSS 33.52.72.13; SNSM 33.61.26.51; Météo 33.22.91.77; Auto 08.36.68.08.50;

FACILITIES
Hérel Marina (850+150 visitors) 33.50.20.06, FF115, Slip, P, D, FW, ME, AC, BH (12 ton), C (10 ton), CH, Gaz, R, V, Bar, SM, El, Sh; **YC de Granville** 33.50.04.25, L, M, BH, D, P, CH, Slip FW, AB, Bar;

Services: CH, M, ME, El, Sh, SHOM, SM.
Town P, D, ME, V, Gaz, R, Bar.
Ferry: UK via Jersey or Cherbourg.

FRANCE - ST. MALO

TIME ZONE –0100
(French Standard Time)
Subtract 1 hour for UT
For French Summer Time add
ONE hour in non-shaded areas

TIMES AND HEIGHTS OF HIGH AND LOW WATERS

MAY

Day	Time	m	Day	Time	m
1 W	0527	10.7	16 TH	0048	2.2
	1219	2.6		0612	11.4
	1753	11.1		1308	2.0
				1830	11.6
2 TH	0036	2.4	17 F	0131	2.0
	0609	11.3		0654	11.6
	1304	2.1		1347	1.9
	1832	11.7		● 1907	11.8
3 F ○	0122	1.8	18 SA	0209	1.9
	0650	11.8		0732	11.6
	1348	1.6		1422	1.8
	1911	12.1		1942	11.8
4 SA	0206	1.4	19 SU	0243	1.8
	0730	12.1		0806	11.6
	1429	1.3		1454	1.9
	1949	12.4		2014	11.7
5 SU	0249	1.1	20 M	0315	1.9
	0810	12.3		0839	11.4
	1508	1.3		1525	2.1
	2027	12.4		2045	11.5
6 M	0329	1.1	21 TU	0346	2.2
	0851	12.2		0911	11.0
	1546	1.5		1556	2.5
	2108	12.2		2116	11.1
7 TU	0409	1.4	22 W	0416	2.7
	0934	11.8		0943	10.6
	1625	1.9		1625	3.0
	2151	11.8		2150	10.6
8 W	0451	1.8	23 TH	0446	3.2
	1020	11.2		1019	10.0
	1708	2.5		1658	3.6
	2238	11.1		2227	10.1
9 TH	0538	2.5	24 F	0521	3.7
	1113	10.5		1100	9.5
	1758	3.1		1738	4.1
	2336	10.4		2312	9.5
10 F	0637	3.1	25 SA	0606	4.1
	1218	9.9		1156	9.0
	1903	3.6		1832	4.5
11 SA	0048	9.9	26 SU	0013	9.0
	0750	3.4		0707	4.4
	1335	9.6		1310	8.8
	2025	3.8		1940	4.6
12 SU	0210	9.8	27 M	0130	8.9
	0911	3.4		0820	4.4
	1455	9.8		1428	9.0
	2147	3.5		2053	4.4
13 M	0328	10.1	28 TU	0245	9.1
	1026	3.0		0933	4.1
	1604	10.3		1532	9.4
	2257	3.0		2200	3.9
14 TU	0432	10.6	29 W	0348	9.7
	1129	2.6		1037	3.6
	1700	10.8		1626	10.1
	2357	2.5		2300	3.3
15 W	0526	11.1	30 TH	0443	10.3
	1223	2.2		1134	2.9
	1748	11.3		1714	10.8
				2357	2.6
			31 F	0533	11.0
				1228	2.3
				1759	11.5

JUNE

Day	Time	m	Day	Time	m
1 SA ○	0051	1.9	16 SU	0143	2.3
	0622	11.6		0711	11.1
	1320	1.7		1357	2.3
	1844	12.1		● 1920	11.5
2 SU	0143	1.4	17 M	0220	2.2
	0709	12.0		0747	11.2
	1408	1.4		1432	2.2
	1929	12.4		1954	11.5
3 M	0233	1.1	18 TU	0255	2.1
	0756	12.3		0821	11.2
	1454	1.2		1506	2.3
	2014	12.6		2027	11.5
4 TU	0320	1.0	19 W	0328	2.2
	0843	12.3		0854	11.0
	1538	1.3		1538	2.4
	2059	12.5		2059	11.3
5 W	0405	1.1	20 TH	0359	2.5
	0930	12.1		0927	10.8
	1622	1.6		1609	2.7
	2146	12.1		2131	11.0
6 TH	0451	1.5	21 F	0430	2.8
	1018	11.6		1001	10.5
	1707	2.1		1640	3.1
	2234	11.6		2206	10.6
7 F	0539	2.0	22 SA	0501	3.2
	1108	11.0		1037	10.0
	1755	2.7		1715	3.5
	2327	10.9		2244	10.1
8 SA	0631	2.6	23 SU	0538	3.6
	1203	10.4		1119	9.6
	1852	3.3		1756	3.9
				2328	9.6
9 SU	0027	10.3	24 M	0622	4.0
	0731	3.2		1211	9.2
	1305	9.9		1847	4.2
	1958	3.7			
10 M	0136	9.9	25 TU	0024	9.2
	0837	3.4		0719	4.2
	1416	9.7		1316	9.0
	2111	3.8		1950	4.3
11 TU	0251	9.8	26 W	0136	9.1
	0947	3.5		0828	4.2
	1527	9.9		1429	9.2
	2221	3.5		2103	4.1
12 W	0400	10.0	27 TH	0251	9.4
	1052	3.2		0943	3.8
	1628	10.3		1536	9.8
	2324	3.2		2215	3.6
13 TH	0458	10.4	28 F	0359	10.0
	1148	3.0		1053	3.2
	1720	10.7		1636	10.5
				2322	2.8
14 F	0017	2.8	29 SA	0501	10.7
	0547	10.7		1157	2.5
	1237	2.7		1731	11.3
	1804	11.0			
15 SA	0103	2.6	30 SU	0024	2.1
	0631	11.0		0559	11.4
	1319	2.5		1256	1.9
	1844	11.3		1824	12.0

JULY

Day	Time	m	Day	Time	m
1 M ○	0124	1.5	16 TU	0202	2.4
	0653	12.0		0730	11.1
	1352	1.4		1415	2.4
	1915	12.5		1937	11.5
2 TU	0220	1.1	17 W	0238	2.2
	0745	12.4		0804	11.2
	1444	1.2		1449	2.3
	2004	12.8		2010	11.6
3 W	0312	0.8	18 TH	0311	2.2
	0835	12.6		0837	11.2
	1532	1.1		1521	2.3
	2051	12.9		2041	11.5
4 TH	0401	0.8	19 F	0342	2.3
	0922	12.5		0908	11.1
	1617	1.3		1551	2.4
	2138	12.6		2112	11.4
5 F	0446	1.1	20 SA	0411	2.5
	1008	12.1		0939	10.9
	1701	1.7		1621	2.6
	2223	12.1		2143	11.0
6 SA	0530	1.7	21 SU	0440	2.8
	1052	11.5		1011	10.6
	1743	2.4		1652	3.0
	2309	11.3		2216	10.6
7 SU	0614	2.4	22 M	0511	3.2
	1138	10.8		1045	10.1
	1829	3.1		1726	3.4
	2358	10.5		2251	10.1
8 M	0700	3.2	23 TU	0547	3.6
	1228	10.1		1124	9.7
	1921	3.8		1808	3.8
				2335	9.6
9 TU	0055	9.8	24 W	0633	4.0
	0755	3.8		1215	9.3
	1329	9.6		1901	4.2
	2025	4.2			
10 W	0206	9.4	25 TH	0037	9.2
	0900	4.1		0735	4.2
	1443	9.4		1329	9.2
	2140	4.2		2012	4.2
11 TH	0325	9.4	26 F	0201	9.2
	1011	4.0		0856	4.1
	1556	9.6		1452	9.5
	2250	3.9		2137	3.8
12 F	0432	9.7	27 SA	0326	9.7
	1115	3.6		1020	3.6
	1655	10.1		1607	10.2
	2349	3.4		2256	3.1
13 SA	0526	10.2	28 SU	0440	10.5
	1210	3.2		1133	2.8
	1743	10.6		1712	11.1
14 SU	0039	3.0	29 M	0006	2.3
	0611	10.6		0544	11.3
	1257	2.8		1238	2.0
	1825	11.1		1810	12.0
15 M	0123	2.6	30 TU	0110	1.5
	0652	10.9		0642	12.0
	1338	2.6		1339	1.4
	● 1902	11.4		○ 1903	12.6
			31 W	0209	0.9
				0734	12.6
				1433	1.0
				1953	13.1

AUGUST

Day	Time	m	Day	Time	m
1 TH	0302	0.6	16 F	0251	2.1
	0823	12.9		0815	11.5
	1522	0.8		1501	2.1
	2040	13.2		2020	11.8
2 F	0350	0.5	17 SA	0320	2.1
	0908	12.9		0845	11.5
	1606	0.9		1531	2.1
	2123	13.0		2050	11.7
3 SA	0432	0.9	18 SU	0349	2.1
	0949	12.5		0914	11.3
	1646	1.4		1600	2.2
	2204	12.4		2119	11.5
4 SU	0511	1.5	19 M	0417	2.4
	1029	11.8		0944	11.1
	1722	2.2		1630	2.5
	2244	11.5		2149	11.0
5 M	0546	2.4	20 TU	0446	2.8
	1106	11.0		1014	10.6
	1758	3.1		1701	3.0
	2324	10.6		2221	10.5
6 TU	0622	3.3	21 W	0519	3.3
	1147	10.1		1048	10.1
	1837	3.9		1738	3.5
				2300	9.9
7 W	0010	9.6	22 TH	0600	3.8
	0706	4.1		1133	9.5
	1238	9.4		1826	4.0
	1933	4.6		2357	9.3
8 TH	0115	9.0	23 F	0657	4.2
	0808	4.6		1244	9.2
	1353	8.9		1935	4.3
	2053	4.8			
9 F	0249	8.8	24 SA	0127	9.1
	0929	4.6		0822	4.3
	1524	9.1		1422	9.3
	2217	4.4		2110	4.0
10 SA	0410	9.2	25 SU	0310	9.5
	1045	4.2		0958	3.8
	1633	9.7		1550	10.0
	2324	3.8		2240	3.3
11 SU	0507	9.9	26 M	0429	10.3
	1146	3.6		1117	2.9
	1723	10.4		1659	11.0
				2353	2.3
12 M	0017	3.2	27 TU	0533	11.3
	0552	10.5		1225	2.1
	1236	3.0		1758	12.0
	1805	10.9			
13 TU	0103	2.7	28 W ○	0058	1.4
	0632	10.9		0628	12.2
	1319	2.6		1325	1.3
	1843	11.4		1850	12.8
14 W	0143	2.4	29 TH	0155	0.8
	0709	11.2		0718	12.8
	1356	2.4		1419	0.8
	● 1918	11.6		1937	13.2
15 TH	0219	2.2	30 F	0246	0.5
	0744	11.4		0803	13.0
	1429	2.2		1506	0.7
	1950	11.8		2021	13.3
			31 SA	0330	0.5
				0845	13.0
				1546	0.8
				2102	13.1

Chart Datum: 6·60 metres below Lallemand System (Mean Sea Level, Marseilles)

ST. MALO

MEAN SPRING
AND NEAP CURVES

MEAN RANGES	
Springs 10.6m	——
Neaps 4.9m	----

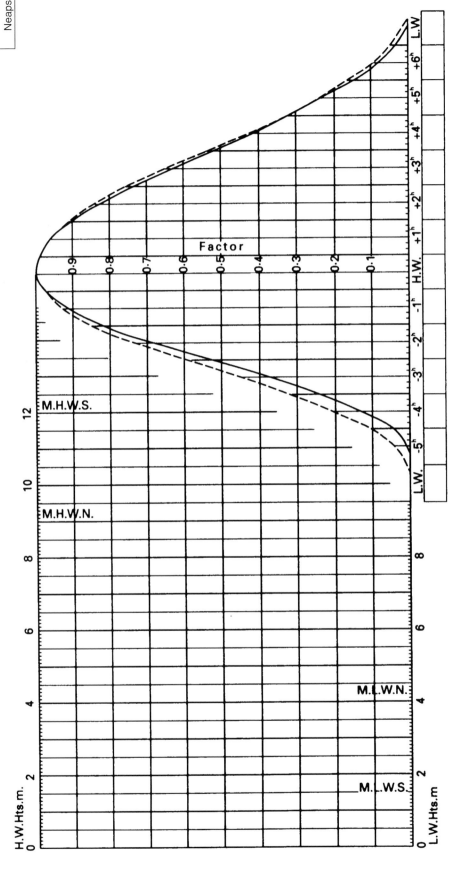

COMPASS DEVIATION TABLE

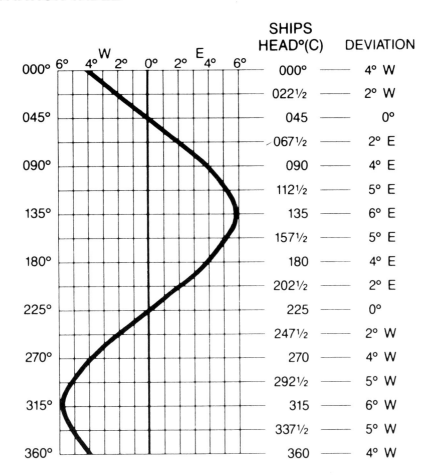

SHIPS HEAD°(C)		DEVIATION
000°	—	4° W
022½	—	2° W
045	—	0°
067½	—	2° E
090	—	4° E
112½	—	5° E
135	—	6° E
157½	—	5° E
180	—	4° E
202½	—	2° E
225	—	0°
247½	—	2° W
270	—	4° W
292½	—	5° W
315	—	6° W
337½	—	5° W
360	—	4° W

Notes

Notes

Notes

RYA Membership

Promoting and Protecting Boating

The RYA is the national organisation which represents the interests of everyone who goes boating for pleasure.

The greater the membership, the louder our voice when it comes to protecting members' interests.

Apply for membership today, and support the RYA, to help the RYA support you.

Benefits of Membership

- Access to expert advice on all aspects of boating from legal wrangles to training matters
- Special members' discounts on a range of products and services including boat insurance, books, videos and class certificates
- Free issue of certificates of competence, increasingly asked for by everyone from overseas governments to holiday companies, insurance underwriters to boat hirers

- Access to the wide range of RYA publications, including the quarterly magazine
- Third Party insurance for windsurfing members
- Free Internet access with RYA-Online
- Special discounts on AA membership
- Regular offers in RYA Magazine
- ...and much more

Join now - membership form overleaf

Join online at *www.rya.org.uk*
or use the form overleaf.
Visit our website for information, advice, members' services and web shop.

Join the RYA now!

1 **Important** To help us comply with Data Protection legislation, please tick *either* Box A or Box B (you must tick Box A to ensure you receive the full benefits of RYA membership). The RYA will not pass your data to third parties.

☐ **A**. I wish to join the RYA and receive future information on member services, benefits (as listed in RYA Magazine and website) and offers.

☐ **B**. I wish to join the RYA but do not wish to receive future information on member services, benefits (as listed in RYA Magazine and website) and offers.

When completed, please send this form to: RYA, RYA House, Ensign Way, Hamble, Southampton, SO31 4YA

2

	Title	Forename	Surname	Date of Birth	Male	Female
1.				D D / M M / Y Y		
2.				D D / M M / Y Y		
3.				D D / M M / Y Y		
4.				D D / M M / Y Y		

Address

Town   County   Post Code

Evening Telephone   Daytime Telephone

email   Signature: _____   Date: _____

3 **Type of membership required:** *(Tick Box)*

☐ **Personal** Current full annual rate £33 or £30 by Direct Debit

☐ **Under 21** Current full annual rate £11 (no reduction for Direct Debit)

☐ **Family*** Current full annual rate £50 or £47 by Direct Debit

* Family Membership: 2 adults plus any under 21s all living at the same address

4 Please tick ONE box to show your main boating interest.

☐ Yacht Racing   ☐ Yacht Cruising
☐ Dinghy Racing   ☐ Dinghy Cruising
☐ Personal Watercraft   ☐ Inland Waterways
☐ Powerboat Racing   ☐ Windsurfing
☐ Motor Boating   ☐ Sportsboats and RIBs

RYA

Instructions to your Bank or Building Society to pay by Direct Debit

Please complete this form and return it to:
Royal Yachting Association, RYA House, Ensign Way, Hamble, Southampton, Hampshire SO31 4YA

DIRECT Debit

To The Manager: Bank/Building Society

Address:

Post Code:

2. Name(s) of account holder(s)

3. Branch Sort Code

☐☐ — ☐☐ — ☐☐

4. Bank or Building Society account number

Originators Identification Number

9	5	5	2	1	3

5. RYA Membership Number (For office use only)

6. Instruction to pay your Bank or Building Society
Please pay Royal Yachting Association Direct Debits from the account detailed in this instruction subject to the safeguards assured by The Direct Debit Guarantee.
I understand that this instruction may remain with the Royal Yachting Association and, if so, details will be passed electronically to my Bank/Building Society.

Signature(s) _____

Date _____

Banks and Building Societies may not accept Direct Debit instructions for some types of account

Cash, Cheque, Postal Order enclosed £ _____
Made payable to the Royal Yachting Association

024	**Office use only:** Membership No Allocated

Office use / Centre Stamp